Classroom Management for Students With Emotional and Behavioral Disorders

This book is dedicated to my wife, Jackie, and my two children, Jacqueline and Scott, who provide me with the love and purpose for undertaking projects that I hope will enhance the lives of others. My life has been blessed by their loving presence. I also dedicate this book to my parents, who provided me with the secure and loving foundation from which to grow; my sister, Carol, who makes me smile and laugh; and my brother-in-law, George, who has always been a positive guiding light in my professional journey.

—*R. P.*

This book is dedicated to my wife, Anita, and two children, Collin and Brittany, who give me the greatest life imaginable. The long hours and many years it took to finish this book would never have been possible without the support of my loving wife. Her constant encouragement, understanding, and love provide me with the strength I need to accomplish my goals. I thank her with all my heart. I also dedicate this book to my parents, who have given me support and guidance throughout my life. Their words of encouragement and guidance have made my professional journey a rewarding and successful experience.

—*G. G.*

A STEP-BY-STEP GUIDE FOR EDUCATORS

Classroom Management for Students With Emotional and Behavioral Disorders

ROGER PIERANGELO ~ GEORGE GIULIANI

CORWIN PRESS
A SAGE Company
Thousand Oaks, CA 91320

For information:

Corwin Press
A SAGE Company
2455 Teller Road
Thousand Oaks, California 91320
www.corwinpress.com

SAGE Ltd.
1 Oliver's Yard
55 City Road
London EC1Y 1SP
United Kingdom

SAGE India Pvt. Ltd.
B 1/I 1 Mohan Cooperative
  Industrial Area
Mathura Road, New Delhi 110 044
India

SAGE Asia-Pacific Pte. Ltd.
33 Pekin Street #02-01
Far East Square
Singapore 048763

Printed in the United States of America.

Library of Congress Cataloging-in-Publication Data

Pierangelo, Roger.
Classroom management for students with emotional and behavioral disorders: a step-by-step guide for educators/Roger Pierangelo and George Giuliani.
    p. cm.
Includes bibliographical references and index.
ISBN 978-1-4129-5426-6 (cloth)
ISBN 978-1-4129-1787-2 (pbk.)
    1. Mentally ill children—Education—United States. 2. Behavior disorders in children—United States. 3. Classroom management—United States.
I. Giuliani, George A., 1938- II. Title.

LC4181.P54 2008
371.94—dc22   2008001266

        10 11 12 10 9 8 7 6 5 4 3 2

Acquisitions Editor:	David Chao
Editorial Assistant:	Mary Dang
Production Editor:	Libby Larson
Copy Editor:	Paula L. Fleming
Typesetter:	C&M Digitals (P) Ltd.
Proofreader:	Charlotte J. Waisner
Cover Designer:	Michael Dubowe
Graphic Designer:	Lisa Riley

Contents

Preface

Who are students with emotional and behavioral disorders? In general, these children and adolescents experience great difficulties in relating appropriately to peers, siblings, parents, and teachers (Jensen, 2005). They also have difficulty responding to academic and social tasks that are essential parts of their schooling. Sometimes they may exhibit too much behavior, or they may be deficient in important academic and social behaviors. In other cases, individuals with emotional or behavioral disorders may not have learned the essential skills necessary for successful participation in school settings (Hardman, Drew, & Egan, 2005).

In defining behavioral disorders or emotional disturbance, no single measure of social or emotional functioning is sufficiently reliable and valid to serve in the way that intelligence tests and other measures do in defining mental retardation and achievement tests in, partially, defining learning disabilities (Rosenberg, Mueser, Jankowski, Salyers, & Acker, 2004). Further, much of the controversy revolves around the ambiguity of the terms used as diagnostic markers and concern that this ambiguity excludes children who require services. For example, phrases such as "inappropriate types of behavior" or "satisfactory interpersonal relationships" are difficult to translate into clear-cut measures of performance. There is also much concern over the exclusion of children identified as "socially maladjusted." The term is considered difficult to define, particularly in view of the possible overlap with behaviors (such as aggression, poor peer relationships) that would qualify a child for special education services.

According to Hunt and Marshall (2005),

the definition of emotional disturbance, like most definitions in special education, is the source of much debate and discussion, and the term "emotional disturbance" is being challenged at the federal level. A number of professionals are urging that the term "emotional or behavioral disorder" be used instead and are also proposing several changes to the definition. Some states have adopted the term "behavior disordered" because of its more direct relationship to assessment and identification procedures.

Classroom Management for Students With Emotional and Behavioral Disorders is intended to provide educators with a step-by-step approach to the most effective methods of teaching students with emotional and behavioral disorders.

Classroom Management for Students With Emotional and Behavioral Disorders was written to explain emotional and behavioral disorders from the eyes of the teacher, so that if a student in your class or school is diagnosed with this disorder, you can work effectively with the administrators, parents, other professionals, and the outside community.

We hope that *Classroom Management for Students With Emotional and Behavioral Disorders* will be helpful to you in understanding the key concepts of emotional and behavioral disorders and how to be an effective educator when working with students diagnosed with them.

Acknowledgments

In the course of writing this book, we have encountered many professional and outstanding Web sites. Those resources have contributed and continue to contribute enormous information, support, guidance, and education to parents, students, and professionals in the area of special education. Although we have accessed many worthwhile sites, we especially thank and acknowledge the National Dissemination Center for Children with Disabilities; the U.S. Department of Education; the National Institutes of Health; the Wisconsin Department of Public Instruction, for providing us with public domain information from *Blueprints for Success: Instructional Strategies to Promote Appropriate Student Behaviors, Child and Adolescent Mental Health Problems—Fact Sheets for School Personnel*, and *DOING IT RIGHT: IEP Goals and Objectives to Address Behavior*; the Minnesota Department of Education, for providing us with public domain information from *Promising Practices in Designing and Using Behavioral Interventions*; and the Colorado Department of Education, for providing us with public domain information from the *Colorado Behavior Resource Manual*.

We would also very much like to thank the professional staff at Corwin Press for its hard work and dedication toward this project. In particular, we thank David Chao, acquisitions editor; Paula Fleming, copyeditor; Libby Larson, production editor; Michael Dubowe, graphic designer; Scott Hooper, print buyer manager; Lisa Riley, production artist; Charlotte Waisner, proofreader; and Mary Dang, editorial assistant.

Roger Pierangelo: I extend thanks to the faculty, administration, and staff of the Department of Graduate Special Education and Literacy at Long Island University; to Ollie Simmons, for her friendship, loyalty, and great personality; to the students and parents of the Herricks

Public Schools whom I have worked with and known over the past 35 years; to the late Bill Smyth, a truly gifted and "extraordinary ordinary" man; and to Helen Firestone, for her influence on my career and her tireless support.

George Giuliani: I extend sincere thanks to all of my colleagues at Hofstra University in the School of Education and Allied Human Services. I am especially grateful to the faculty and staff at Hofstra University, including Maureen Murphy (dean), Darra Pace (chairperson), Frank Bowe, Diane Schwartz (graduate program director of early childhood special education), Mary McDonald, Elfreda Blue, Gloria Wilson, Daniel Sciarra, Laurie Johnson, Joan Bloomgarden, Jamie Mitus, Estelle Gellman, Holly Seirup, Andrea Perkins, Genevieve Weber, Deborah Elkis-Abuhoff, Sage Rose, Donna Levinson, Adele Piombino, Marjorie Butler, Ann Tarantino, and Eve Byrne. I also thank my brother and sister, Roger and Claudia; my mother-in-law, Ursula Jenkeleit; my sisters in-law, Karen and Cindy; and my brothers-in-law, Robert and Bob. They have provided me with encouragement and reinforcement in all of my personal and professional endeavors.

About the Authors

Dr. Roger Pierangelo, PhD, is an associate professor in the Department of Special Education and Literacy at Long Island University. He has been an administrator of special education programs; served for 18 years as a permanent member of Committees on Special Education; has over 30 years of experience in the public school system as a general education classroom teacher and school psychologist; and serves as a consultant to numerous private and public schools, PTA, and SEPTA groups. Dr. Pierangelo has also been an evaluator for the New York State Office of Vocational and Rehabilitative Services and a director of a private clinic. He is a New York State–licensed clinical psychologist, a certified school psychologist, and a Board Certified Diplomate Fellow in Student and Adolescent Psychology and Forensic Psychology. Dr. Pierangelo is the executive director of the National Association of Special Education Teachers (NASET) and an executive director of the American Academy of Special Education Professionals (AASEP). He also holds the office of vice president of the National Association of Parents with Children in Special Education (NAPCSE).

Dr. Pierangelo earned his BS from St. John's University, MS from Queens College, Professional Diploma from Queens College, PhD from Yeshiva University, and Diplomate Fellow in Student and Adolescent Psychology and Forensic Psychology from the International College of Professional Psychology. Dr. Pierangelo is a member of the American Psychological Association, New York State Psychological Association, Nassau County Psychological Association, New York State Union of Teachers, and Phi Delta Kappa.

Dr. Pierangelo is the author of multiple books by Corwin Press, including *The Big Book of Special Education Resources* and the *Step-by-Step Guide for Educators* series.

Dr. George Giuliani, JD, PsyD, is a full-time tenured associate professor and the director of Special Education at Hofstra University's School of Education and Allied Human Services in the Department of Counseling, Research, Special Education, and Rehabilitation. Dr. Giuliani earned his BA from the College of the Holy Cross, MS from St. John's University, JD from City University Law School, and PsyD from Rutgers University, the Graduate School of Applied and Professional Psychology. He earned Board Certification as a Diplomate Fellow in Student and Adolescent Psychology and Forensic Psychology from the International College of Professional Psychology. Dr. Giuliani is also a New York State–licensed psychologist and certified school psychologist and has an extensive private practice focusing on students with special needs. He is a member of the American Psychological Association, New York State Psychological Association, National Association of School Psychologists, Suffolk County Psychological Association, Psi Chi, American Association of University Professors, and the Council for Exceptional Students.

Dr. Giuliani is the president of the National Association of Parents with Children in Special Education (NAPCSE), executive director of the National Association of Special Education Teachers (NASET), and executive director of the American Academy of Special Education Professionals (AASEP). He is a consultant for school districts and early childhood agencies and has provided numerous workshops for parents and guardians and teachers on a variety of special education and psychological topics. Dr. Giuliani is the coauthor of numerous books by Corwin Press, including *The Big Book of Special Education Resources* and the *Step-by-Step Guide for Educators* series.

Step I

Review Your Knowledge of Students With Emotional and/or Behavioral Disorders

Definition of Emotional Disturbance

Our nation's federal law in special education is the Individuals With Disabilities Education Improvement Act of 2004 (Individuals with Disabilities Act [IDEA], 2004). Under IDEA 2004, an emotional disturbance is defined as

(i) a condition exhibiting one or more of the following characteristics over a long period of time and to a marked degree that adversely affects a child's educational performance:

    (a) An inability to learn that cannot be explained by intellectual, sensory, or health factors.

    (b) An inability to build or maintain satisfactory interpersonal relationships with peers and teachers.

    (c) Inappropriate types of behavior or feelings under normal circumstances.

(d) A general pervasive mood of unhappiness or depression.

(e) A tendency to develop physical symptoms or fears associated with personal or school problems.

(ii) Emotional disturbance includes schizophrenia. The term does not apply to children who are socially maladjusted, unless it is determined that they have an emotional disturbance. . . . (IDEA, 2004)

Causes of Emotional and Behavioral Disorders

The causes of emotional and behavioral disorders have not been adequately determined. However, research suggests that emotional disturbances are caused by a combination of biological, psychological, and environmental factors.

Imbalance of Neurotransmitters

Some types of mental illnesses have been linked to an abnormal balance of special chemicals in the brain called neurotransmitters. A neurotransmitter is a chemical that helps transmit nerve impulses through the nervous system. The body uses many different neurotransmitters, and these can have an adverse affect on the individual's mental state (Kirk, Gallagher, & Anastasiow, 2003). For example, the neurotransmitter chemicals norepinephrine, serotonin, acetylcholine, dopamine, and gamma-aminobutryric acid seem to be lower in some depressed people or higher in nondepressed people (Harper, 2003). If these chemicals are out of balance or are not working properly, messages may not make it through the brain correctly, leading to symptoms of mental illness.

Genetics (Heredity)

Many mental illnesses run in families, suggesting that people who have a family member with a mental illness are more susceptible (have a greater likelihood of being affected) to developing a mental illness. Susceptibility is passed on in families through genes. Experts believe many mental illnesses are linked to abnormalities in many genes, not just one (Kauffman, 2005). That is why a person can inherit a susceptibility to a mental illness but not necessarily develop the illness. Mental illness itself occurs from the interaction of multiple genes and other factors such as stress, abuse, or a traumatic event that can influence, or trigger, an illness in a person who has an inherited susceptibility to it (Jensen, 2005).

Infections

Certain infections have been linked to brain damage and the development of mental illness or the worsening of its symptoms. For example, a condition known as pediatric autoimmune neuropsychiatric disorder associated with the *Streptococcus* bacterium has been linked to the development of obsessive-compulsive disorder and other mental illnesses in children (Cleveland Clinic Department of Psychiatry and Psychology, 2005).

Brain Defects or Injury

Defects in or injury to certain areas of the brain have been linked to some mental illnesses (Jensen, 2005; Kauffman, 2005).

Prenatal Damage

Some evidence suggests that a disruption of early fetal brain development or trauma that occurs at the time of birth—for example, loss of oxygen to the brain—may be a factor in the development of certain conditions such as autism (Cleveland Clinic Department of Psychiatry and Psychology, 2005; Kauffman, 2005).

Other Factors

Poor nutrition and exposure to toxins, such as lead, may play a role in the development of mental illnesses (Jensen, 2005; Kauffman, 2005).

Psychological Factors That May Result in Mental Illness

A number of psychological factors may contribute to an emotional or behavioral disorder (Gargiulo, 2004; Hallahan & Kauffman, 2006; Jensen, 2005; Kauffman, 2005):

- Dysfunctional family life
- Early loss of an important person, such as the loss of a parent
- Educational failure
- Emotional, physical, or educational neglect

- Feelings of inadequacy, low self-esteem, anxiety, anger, or loneliness
- High levels of stress
- Poor relations with peers and adults
- Substance abuse
- Trauma experienced as a child, such as emotional, physical, or sexual abuse

Prevalence of Emotional Disturbance

According to the *Twenty-Sixth Annual Report* (U.S. Department of Education, 2004), 482,597 students between 6 and 21 years of age were identified as having emotional disturbances. This represents slightly more than 8 percent of all students having a classification in special education, or less than 1 percent of all school-age students.

Age of Onset of Emotional and Behavioral Disorders

There is relatively little emotional disturbance reported in the early grades, with a sharp increase and peak during the middle grades and a decline in prevalence beginning in middle school and continuing through high school (U.S. Department of Education, 2004).

Gender Features of Emotional and Behavioral Disorders

Males are significantly more likely than females to fall within each major disability group. The largest disparity is within the category of emotional disturbance, where boys comprise some 80 percent of the population. Among the general population of students in Grades 1 to 8, there are more boys with emotional disturbance (7 percent of all boys in special education are classified as emotionally disturbed) than girls (4 percent of all girls in special education are so classified). Sources document that boys outnumber girls about five to one (Hallahan & Kauffman, 2006; Hardman, Drew, & Egan, 2005; Heward, 2006; Turnbull, Turnbull, Shank, & Smith, 2004).

Cultural Features of Emotional and Behavioral Disorders

According to Turnbull et al. (2004),

> African American males are overrepresented in the category of emotional or behavioral disorders. The special education community faces three challenges in terms of this high identification rate: (1) unavailability of culturally appropriate assessment instruments, (2) concern about teacher expectations regarding appropriate behavior, and (3) building respectful family-professional partnerships that may prevent identification. Ethnically diverse groups are more likely to experience stressors such as "poverty, discrimination, violence, violent death, drug and alcohol abuse, and teenage pregnancy" that can contribute to mental health problems. (p. 144)

Although African Americans comprise 14.8 percent of the school population, they comprise nearly 27 percent of the students who receive special education services due to having an emotional disturbance (U.S. Department of Education, 2004).

Eligibility Criteria for Emotional Disturbance Under IDEA

In determining eligibility under IDEA, the individualized education program (IEP) team must decide if a student has an emotional condition that is manifested by one or more of the five characteristics listed in the definition of emotional disturbance. These characteristics must meet the qualifying conditions of adverse effect on educational performance occurring over a long period of time (chronicity) and to a marked degree (severity):

- *Long period of time.* The standard for duration is not precisely specified. The literature frequently makes reference to several months as an appropriate standard. The intention is to avoid labeling a student who is temporarily reacting to a situational trauma. The characteristics must also be evident over time and situations (Connecticut State Department of Education, 1997).

- *Marked degree.* The problems are significant and apparent to school staff members who observe the student in a variety of settings and situations. A comparison is made with the student's appropriate peer group; the problems must be more severe or frequent than the normally expected range of behavior for individuals of the same age, gender, and cultural group. The characteristics must be persistent and generalized across environments (Connecticut State Department of Education, 1997).

Characteristics of Students With Emotional Disturbance

The causes of emotional disturbance have not been adequately determined. Although various factors such as heredity, brain disorder, diet, stress, and family functioning have been suggested as possible causes, research has not shown any of these factors to be a direct cause of behavioral or emotional problems (Jensen, 2005). Some of the characteristics and behaviors seen in children who have emotional disturbances include the following:

- Hyperactivity (short attention span, impulsiveness)
- Aggression or self-injurious behavior (acting out, fighting); tendency of classmates to reject them (Bullis, Walker, & Sprague, 2001)
- Withdrawal (failure to initiate interaction with others, retreat from exchanges of social interaction, excessive fear or anxiety)
- Immaturity (inappropriate crying, temper tantrums, poor coping skills)
- Learning difficulties (academically performing below grade level)

Children with the most serious emotional disturbances may exhibit distorted thinking, excessive anxiety, bizarre motor acts, and abnormal mood swings. Some are identified as having a severe psychosis or schizophrenia (Jensen, 2005).

Many children who do not have emotional disturbances may display some of these same behaviors at various times during their development. However, when children have an emotional disturbance, these behaviors continue over long periods of time. Their behavior thus signals that they are not coping with their environment or peers (Turnbull et al., 2004).

Possibly more than any other group of children with disabilities, children with emotional or behavior disorders present problems with social skills to themselves, their families, their peers, and their teachers (U.S. Department of Education, 2001).

Children With Emotional Disturbances and School-Related Concerns

School failure is the common link between delinquency and disability (Office of Special Education Programs (OSEP), 2001, p. II-3). Regardless of intellectual potential, students with emotional or behavioral disorders typically do not perform well academically.

Educational programs for children with an emotional disturbance need to include attention to providing emotional and behavioral support as well as helping them master academics; develop social skills; and increase self-awareness, self-control, and self-esteem. A large body of research exists regarding methods of providing students with positive behavioral support (PBS) in the school environment so that problem behaviors are minimized and positive, appropriate behaviors are fostered (Heward, 2006; Hunt & Marshall, 2005; Turnbull et al., 2004). It is also important to know that within the school setting, the following are taking place:

- For a child whose behavior impedes learning (including the learning of others), the team developing the child's IEP considers, if appropriate, strategies to address that behavior, including positive behavioral interventions, strategies, and supports.
- Students eligible for special education services under the category of emotional disturbance may have IEPs that include psychological or counseling services. These important related services must be available under law and be provided by a qualified social worker, psychologist, guidance counselor, or other qualified personnel.
- Career education (both vocational and academic) is a major part of secondary education and should be a part of the transition plan included in every adolescent's IEP.

There is growing recognition that families, as well as their children, need support, respite care, intensive case management, and a collaborative, multiagency approach to services. Many communities are working toward providing such wraparound services. A growing

number of agencies and organizations is actively involved in establishing support services in the community (National Dissemination
Center for Children with Disabilities (NICHCY), 2004).

IDEA Exclusion of Students Who Are "Socially Maladjusted"

Students who are "socially maladjusted" do not qualify for special
education under IDEA unless they meet the criteria for an emotional
disturbance in another way. Social maladjustment without a linkage
to an emotional disorder is often characterized by deviant behavior
with conscious control. Emotional overreactions may occur when the
behavior is criticized or punishment is applied. Anger is a frequent
reaction, but the thoughts are related to the situation.

The student's perceptions are logically related to the situation and
consistent with other people's perceptions (Hallahan & Kauffman,
2006; Jensen, 2005). The following indicators are often associated with
a social maladjustment rather than an emotional disorder:

- Signs of depression may be present but are not pervasive.
- Problem behaviors are goal directed, self-serving, and manipulative.
- Actions are based on perceived self-interest, even though
  others may consider the behavior to be self-defeating.
- Inappropriate behaviors are displayed in selected settings or
  situations (for example, only at home, in school, or in selected
  classes), while most behavior is controlled.
- Problem behaviors are frequently exhibited by and encouraged
  by the peer group, and the actions are intentional with understanding of the consequences.
- General social conventions and behavioral standards are
  understood but are not accepted; countercultural standards of
  the neighborhood and peers are accepted and followed.
- Problem behaviors have escalated during preadolescence
  or adolescence (Hallahan & Kauffman, 2006; Jensen, 2005;
  Kauffman, 2005).

The exclusion of students who are socially maladjusted but not emotionally disturbed is one of the most heavily criticized parts of IDEA's
definition of an emotional disturbance (Hallahan & Kauffman, 2006).

Step II

Understand the Behaviors of Students With Emotional and/or Behavioral Disorders

Understanding Challenging Behaviors

Great strides have been taken in the education of children with disabilities since the enactment of P.L. 94-142, the Education of the Handicapped Act (EHA). However, areas of concern remain. The federal definition refers to special education as "specially designed instruction, at no cost to parents, to meet the *unique needs of a child* [emphasis added] with a disability" (34 CFR 300.17[a]). Too often, however, when working with students with challenging behaviors, methodology has focused more on controlling behavior than on addressing the *needs* underlying the behavior and instruction toward more appropriate ways of getting those needs met.

Challenging Behaviors Serve a Function for the Student

Challenging behaviors (or sets or chains of behaviors) are always directed at achieving a desired outcome. In essence, such behaviors exist because they serve a useful purpose for the student. The behavior has worked in some way to meet a need for the student in the past, and the student will continue to use it because it has worked.

Although challenging behaviors may be socially inappropriate, from the student's perspective, they are reasonable and logical responses to events that have occurred in their environment (e.g., responses to a reprimand, teacher direction, or a bad headache).

Many students with significant skill deficits use challenging behaviors because they have no other means for successfully influencing their environment or communicating their needs. Challenging behaviors may be viewed as basic forms of communication (e.g., crying to indicate hunger) or social interaction (e.g., clowning around to initiate social interactions). Other, more socially skilled students use challenging behaviors because they are the most efficient or effective way to achieve a desired outcome.

Functions of behavior can be divided roughly according to two purposes: "to get something" or "to avoid or escape something." When a student's behavior functions to get something, it means that the student's teacher or peers respond to a challenging behavior by giving the student attention, approval, or tangibles. For example, name-calling may result in giggles from peers, acting out may result in a trip to the gym to "cool off," or scribbling on class work may result in extra teacher assistance on a worksheet.

When a student's challenging behavior functions to avoid or escape something, it means that the teacher or peers respond to a challenging behavior by stopping an event that the student finds unpleasant. For example, whining and complaining after each direction may result in a teacher's lessening demands, or threatening to hit a peer may result in the cessation of teasing.

It is important to note that the form of behavior (how a student acts) is not necessarily related to function. For example, a student may say, "Leave me alone," in an effort to bring greater teacher attention (e.g., the teacher responds by saying, "Come on. You don't really mean that. Let's do . . ."). It is impossible to identify function accurately just by describing student actions. Function can only be determined by describing student's interactions within the environment.

Challenging Behaviors Are Context Related

A behavior occurs because of what precedes or follows it. Challenging behaviors do not occur in a vacuum but rather because certain environmental or ecological variables have induced them to occur. These variables can be identified through careful analysis and assessment.

Several general classes of context variables influence behaviors. One such class is *immediate antecedents*, referring to events that occur just prior to the challenging behavior. Such events trigger an immediate reaction from the student. Examples of immediate antecedents include a teacher direction, a difficult work task, a reprimand, or peer teasing.

Setting events is a second general class and refers to context variables that occur concurrently with the behavior of concern or at an earlier time. Setting events work to "set the stage" for a challenging behavior to occur. They include setting characteristics such as seating arrangements or the schedule of classroom activities; prior social interactions such as a fight on the bus on the way to school; and physical conditions of the student such as illness, fatigue, or allergies.

Another, broader class of context variables that influence behaviors is *lifestyle factors.* Although often difficult to identify precisely, such factors contribute to the overall quality of one's life. The presence or absence of such factors as participation in personally meaningful activities, the opportunity for choice and control, inclusion in typical school and community activities, friendships, and good relationships with family members and others can have a profound influence on the behaviors that students exhibit day to day. Because positive life experiences provide the motivation for learning, they are necessary conditions for the success of behavioral support and interventions.

Effective Interventions Are Based on a Thorough Understanding of the Challenging Behavior

Effective interventions result in long-term behavioral change. To produce long-term results, effective interventions must directly address the function and contextual influences of the challenging behavior. Once challenging behaviors are understood in terms of the outcomes they produce for a student, the goal is to replace challenging behaviors with socially acceptable alternatives that will help the student to achieve the same outcomes. If challenging behaviors reflect a skill deficit, then the solution is to teach acceptable alternatives. Interventions that ignore function by simply trying to suppress (e.g., punish) a behavior are likely to fail because the student's needs remain unmet. Even students who know how to behave appropriately, but do not, can benefit from instruction. Students can learn that appropriate behaviors are effective and efficient means for achieving desired results.

For Example:

- *A student stops working and starts talking to classmates.* The teacher might assume that the student is being noncompliant. If the teacher can recognize that the student is anxious because the lesson is not understood, the teacher can teach the student to recognize and express the need for help and to ask for and obtain assistance.
- *A student puts his head down on his or her desk.* The teacher might assume that the student is being disrespectful. However, if the teacher knows that the student typically puts his head down when he has a headache, the teacher might ask him if his head hurts, teach him to express his need, and allow him either to see the school nurse or to leave his head down until he feels better (Topper, Williams, Leo, Hamilton, & Fox, 1994).

Effective interventions also address the contextual influences of behavior. Once the contextual influences of a challenging behavior are understood, the goal is to prevent that behavior from occurring by changing the environment. Prevention strategies can be as simple as modifying an assignment or changing the pace of instruction to avoid student frustration, or they can be as complex as modifying morning routines at home or learning experiences at school to match student needs. Interventions that focus on changing the student's behavior without also addressing the behavior's contextual influences are likely to fail because the student's situation (the one that produces the challenging behavior) remains unchanged.

Understand the Difference Between Symptoms and Problems

One of the most important concepts to know when working with children with emotional disturbances is the difference between a symptom and a problem. Understanding this difference will be crucial when it comes time to develop a treatment plan or a functional behavioral assessment. Many times, teachers will mistake a symptom for a problem and miss the opportunity to identify the real issues in a more timely manner.

As emotional problems (e.g., conflicts, fears, insecurities, vulnerabilities) develop, the pressure from these issues forms tension. This tension can only be released in one of two ways: verbally or behaviorally. If the children are unable to label their feelings correctly, then the tension will vent in behavior, or what we call behavioral symptoms. That is why counseling or therapy can be beneficial to a child, because part of the process involves identifying and labeling conflicts so that the child can talk out the tension.

Usually, the more serious the problem(s), the greater the level of tension. A high level of tension will need to be released through several symptomatic behaviors. Therefore, the more serious the problem(s), the greater frequency, intensity, and duration of the behavioral symptoms. Further, high levels of tension result in more immediate behavioral symptoms. As a result, the behaviors may be inappropriate and impulsive rather than well thought out.

As the child becomes more confident or learns to work out problems (e.g, through therapy, classroom management, intervention strategies, etc.), the underlying problems become smaller. What results is a decrease in the levels of tension and consequently lower frequency, intensity, and duration of the inappropriate, impulsive, or self-destructive behavior patterns.

Normally, these behavioral symptoms are the first signal noticed by teachers, parents, and professionals. If this pattern is not fully understood, both the child and the teacher will become very frustrated during attempts to extinguish the symptoms. Identifying symptoms as indicators of something more serious is another first step in helping children work out their problems.

Behaviors That May
Be Indicative of More Serious Problems

Examples of typical symptomatic behavior patterns that may be indicative of more serious problems may include the following:

- Anxiety
- Constantly blames others for problems
- Controlling
- Defies authority
- Distractible
- Fearful of adults
- Fearful of new situations
- Fears criticism
- Gives many excuses for inappropriate behavior
- Hyperactive
- Impulsivity

- Inflexibility
- Intrusive
- Irresponsibility
- Moody
- Overly critical
- Overreactive
- Panics easily
- Physical with others
- Poor judgment
- Procrastinates
- Rarely takes chances
- Short attention span
- Tires easily
- Unable to focus on task
- Verbally hesitant

Once these behaviors are noticed, the teacher should evaluate the seriousness of the situation by applying three rules (Pierangelo, 2004).

1. *What is the frequency of the symptoms?* Consider how often the symptoms occur. The more serious the problem, the greater amount of tension generated. The greater the amount of tension, the more frequent will be the need to release it. Therefore, the greater the frequency of the symptom, the greater chance that the problem(s) are serious and should be handled immediately with the help of the special education teacher or psychologist.

2. *What is the duration of the symptoms?* The more serious the problem, the greater the degree of tension generated. The greater the degree of tension, the longer the student will need to release it. Therefore, the longer the duration of the symptoms, the more serious the problem.

3. *What is the intensity of the symptoms?* The more serious the problem, the more intense the level of resulting tension will be. This level of tension will require a more intense release.

Symptomatic Behaviors Exhibited When a Child Has Low Levels of Tension

When students possess low levels of tension, they exhibit what are called positive behavior symptoms more often than not. In school, for instance, the child will exhibit (more often than not) behaviors that include the following:

- Adequate organizational skills
- Age-appropriate attention span
- Appropriate memory
- Consistency
- Flexibility
- Good concentration
- Responsibility with school work

Parents will see positive behavior symptoms resulting from low levels of tension such as the following:

- Appropriate judgment
- No problems falling asleep
- Normal strivings for parental approval
- Resiliency
- Willingness to reason
- Willingness to try

Again, keep in mind that these patterns may vary to some degree during adolescence and still be within normal limits.

Socially, children with low tension levels will (more often than not) be able to

- maintain social interactions;
- show willingness to try new social experiences; and
- treat peers appropriately.

Symptomatic Behaviors Exhibited
When a Child Has High Levels of Tension

However, according to Pierangelo and Giuliani (2006), when serious conflicts arise, the available energy must be drained away to deal with the conflicts like white blood cells to an infection. Because energy must be drained away, less energy is available to keep things in perspective and maintain consistency. When you observe a pattern of behavior that is inappropriate and results in serious symptoms, you should automatically become aware that some serious problem may exist.

When a child has high levels of tension, negative behavior patterns will be exhibited. When this occurs, the negative patterns may show up at school in the following ways:

- Disorganization
- Inability to focus on task
- Inflexibility
- Irresponsibility
- Procrastination
- Projecting the reasons for problems on everyone and everything else

A parent may observe negative behavior patterns at home such as the following:

- Forgetfulness
- Overreactions
- Oversensitivity
- Unwillingness to reason
- Unwillingness to venture out

When high levels of tension exist, they may interfere in social functioning. For example, one may observe the student

- withdrawing from social situations;
- constantly finding fault with peers;
- being unwilling to try new social experiences; or
- express social fears or beliefs that no one likes him or her.

If therapy is required, be aware that it can be a long-term process, especially if the problems have been around for a long time. Consequently, the treatment approach may need to combine outside therapy, family therapy, and classroom behavior management. After these interventions have taken place, you can tell if your student is making progress by the reduction of the frequency, intensity, and duration of the negative symptomatic behavior patterns. Also, be aware that some parents may resist therapy, leaving your classroom management techniques as the only intervention strategy. These will be discussed in further chapters.

Redirecting Students to More Appropriate Behaviors

Many approaches may be effective in redirecting students to more appropriate behaviors when a challenging situation appears to be developing. The goal for educators is to help the student decrease emotional intensity while conveying that they are there to support the student and to understand why the student is having a hard time. Adults who are successful at supporting a student through a difficult time are seen by the student as unconditionally caring, trustworthy, able to protect them from harm and humiliation, confident that the student can cope with excessive stress, and confident that the future will be better.

The following techniques and strategies are offered as options for redirecting students to more appropriate behaviors. *It is important to tailor interventions to the developmental level of the student.* These options are not intended to be the sole interventions to increase a positive behavior; rather, they are examples of how inappropriate behaviors may be de-escalated or redirected so as to avoid the need for more intrusive interventions.

As with all interventions, teams will want to choose techniques and strategies that support the return of the student to appropriate behaviors rather than approaches that inadvertently reinforce negative behaviors.

Interest Boosting

When students' behavior indicates that they are drifting away from attending to the task or activity, some additional information related to their interests or experiences is helpful to pique their attention or interest in the activity. For example, when leading a discussion about music, the staff member might ask the students about their personal stereo equipment to boost their interest in the discussion.

Planned Ignoring

This technique is more successful if planned before the behavior occurs. It is most effective when a student is trying to get attention or to provoke staff members, as long as other students are not involved. Not calling on the student to run an errand or ignoring the student while telling several other students what a good job they are doing are examples of this technique. It is important to provide a positive reinforcer as soon as an appropriate behavior is exhibited; be ready to reinforce the correct behavior the moment it appears. Do not use this technique for severe behavior problems. "Remember that there is a qualitative difference between ignoring a person's behavior and ignoring a person. Find a way to minimize attention given to a behavior and continue to offer support" (Topper et al., 1994).

Providing More Information

Clarifying expectations and experiences in a form compatible with the person's assessed learning style helps to ensure that the student is not reacting to some misunderstanding or misperception of the activity or interaction (see Boeckmann, Cardelli, and Jacobs, 1989).

Tension Reduction Through Humor

Frequently, a problem or potential problem may be defused with a joke or a lighthearted comment. Many times, anxiety, fear, or a challenge will make the student feel obligated or forced to react negatively. Humor can act as a pressure release valve to allow the student to laugh off something without a negative response—to "save face," in other words. This technique may be effective when the student has responded instinctively in a negative fashion or appears to be wanting to retaliate but is indecisive concerning whether or how to do so. Never use satire or ridicule and be aware if student "reads" an attempt at humor as ridicule; the student must correctly read the caring aspect of the interaction.

Acknowledging the Message

Acknowledging, in a nonjudgmental fashion, the message or emotion expressed through a challenging behavior, even when we are unable to honor the message or condone its form, can serve as a prelude to other strategies and help set the stage for a successful and respectful outcome (e.g., "I know it is hard to wait your turn . . ."). Acknowledgment may also help to teach the "right words to say" by positively restating the person's behaviorally expressed message (Boeckmann et al., 1989).

Signal Interference

This technique includes signaling the student with nonverbal indications when behavior is beginning to be inappropriate (e.g., snapping fingers, holding up hand to indicate "stop"). This is most useful for behaviors that are mild in nature when they have just begun to escalate.

Proximity Control

When a student's behavior is beginning to be disruptive or distracting, the staff member moves close to the student while carrying on the activity with the whole group. No punishment or undue attention is given to the student at the time. Generally, the adult's presence at close range is enough to subdue mild inappropriate behaviors. Be attentive to whether the student may perceive proximity as a threat.

Hurdle Help

A staff member provides immediate instruction at the very moment the student experiences trouble to help him or her over the hurdle of dealing appropriately with others. A timely comment at the onset of the problem may help the student follow the correct course of action. For example, when a staff member sees a student bunching up a piece of paper and preparing to throw it, the staff member reminds the student to walk to the trash can to throw it away. Timing is essential with this strategy.

Restructuring Routine

While routine has a stabilizing effect on everyone, sometimes students tire of it. Adjusting to energy level provides the opportunity for a student to be refreshed. Shifts in routine should be occasional so as not to disrupt the orderliness of a planned, sequenced routine (e.g., rescheduling TV time to allow students to watch a special program after the group has completed tasks). Note that students with severe behavior problems may require visual reminders of routines, such as personal schedules of their activities on their desks. Changes should be explained and integrated into any visual tracking system the student is using.

Making a Direct Appeal to Values

Students are encouraged to make a decision as to whether their behavior is helping the situation. One-on-one conferencing may elicit an understanding of how the behavior may be making matters worse and to discover alternate behaviors that can help the students focus on the matter at hand and their part in it. A questioning format is most effective here, beginning with questions that require a yes answer (to develop a positive attitude) and phasing in questions that require a more involved answer (e.g., Where did this happen? What did you do then? How do you feel about that? Why do you think you responded in this way?). Finally, seek out some sort of commitment for continuing a behavior or stopping a behavior next time the problem occurs.

Distraction

When a confrontation or a negative behavior is creating a disturbance, focusing the group's attention and/or the individual's attention on something different can reduce or eliminate the problem. A student who is screaming may stop to listen if the staff member begins discussing a topic of interest to the student or if the staff member begins an activity with the other students that the student would enjoy. This technique helps the student to give up the negative behavior by providing an opportunity to make the choice to do so and prevents the staff member from having to use more restrictive interventions.

Infusion With Affection

Often a very positive, supportive, and appreciative approach may help a student to respond more appropriately. A warm, open, caring response from a staff member may help the student talk about the problems being experienced before the problems build into a significant incident. An example might be, "I think you probably feel very sad now, and that makes me feel bad, too. Do you think we might walk and be able to talk about what happened?"

Regrouping

When a student is having trouble within a group, it is often helpful to move the student to another group or space to avoid continuing problems. This is not a punishing "kick-out" but an attempt to offer the student an environment that will help the child maintain control of the behavior. For example, "I think this new location will be better for you and allow you to be in control of yourself. I can see you're trying."

The Antiseptic Bounce

When a student's behavior indicates a build-up of stress or restlessness, it may be helpful to remove the student in such a way that attention is not focused on the negative behavior. For example, a pass to the office to run an errand may be enough to defuse a potential problem and allow the student to return fresh to the activity. This allows a few minutes away from the problem area without confrontation about behavior and may provide enough of a release and a distraction to enable the student to return to the program in a new frame of mind.

Limiting Supplies and Materials

When a student begins to misuse, abuse, or otherwise cause a problem with tools or supplies, it may be advisable to limit continuing access to the material at that time. This requires a calm voice and a supportive stance if de-escalation is desired.

Interpretation As Interference

A student may not understand or be aware of a behavior that is occurring. Sometimes it may be helpful to describe to students what they are doing by commenting on observable behavior. This technique serves as a reminder that the behavior is inappropriate. For example, "When you talk while I am talking, not only is it hard for you to listen, but it is hard for others to listen, too."

Being a Role Model

The most significant management tool available to staff members is conducting themselves in the manner in which students are expected to behave. Staff members who demonstrate self-control, respect for others, good manners, courtesy, honesty, fairness, and good judgment teach by example. Students with serious behavior issues often attend to the emotional tone of the speaker with more concentration than they give to the actual words. Clear, calm words may be modeled by other students and immediately diffuse a tense situation. For example, "Mrs. Walsh says it's not my job to worry about Johnny. My job is _____ right now."

Pacing Indicator

Some students, especially those with severe disabilities, lose the ability of language when protesting an activity choice. Shifting the student to "break time" and asking the student to rejoin the instructional activity when ready can be effective in diffusing escalating behaviors. For example, giving a student an object that signifies break time (e.g., a magazine, small stuffed animal, a felt heart), to be returned when the student is ready, may de-escalate behavior and provide for choice making.

More Tips on Neutralizing or Momentarily Calming the Immediate Situation

1. Think about what message you are communicating by
   - your position and proximity to the student (e.g., avoid being a threat, avoid chasing, avoid getting hurt, keep the student safe);
   - how quickly or slowly you are talking or moving;

- your tone of voice;
- the intensity of your response (e.g., if the student is loud, then you need to be calm and quiet).

2. Try not to focus on the struggle; think about what you want the student to do instead (i.e., ideally what the situation should look like).

3. Take into consideration that the student may be scared, confused, and embarrassed and may need to "save face." Provide a fair and logical option to calm the moment.

4. Whenever possible, continue the flow of the day. This will minimize focusing on the "problem behavior."

5. When safety is an issue, interrupt the behavior to avoid injury but do so by supporting, not punishing, the person.

6. Remember there is a qualitative difference between ignoring a person's behavior and ignoring a person.

7. If necessary, adjust the environment to keep things from getting worse.

8. If you think your response is making things worse, stop and re-evaluate.

9. Others should continue with their regular day—if you need help, tell others what they should do. If another teacher is dealing with a difficult situation, refrain from intervening unless asked to do so (Topper et al., 1994).

Ways to Maintain Positive Changes in Student Behavior

The success of any plan to change student behaviors depends on the willingness and ability of the student to continue to use the appropriate behavior without excessive outside support (i.e., the intervention). The most basic way to ensure maintenance of behavior change is to be sure that interventions teach the student a set of skills. Teaching skills requires IEP teams to include strategies in the behavioral intervention plan to teach the student in such a way as to promote the maintenance (i.e., lasting over time, even when the extrinsic reinforcers have faded) and generalization (i.e., using the behavior in other appropriate settings) of replacement behaviors. One strategy for doing this is to restructure the social environment to leverage the power of peer relationships to promote positive behavior. These behaviors are then maintained though the natural consequences of having and being with friends. Indeed, in numerous instances, students have been taught to encourage or reinforce appropriate behavior and to ignore or walk away from negative provocations of their classmates.

Another way to promote long-lasting behavior change is to use strategies based on cognitive mediation (i.e., thinking through a situation before acting on emotion) and self-management (i.e., using techniques to control one's own behavior). For example, students have been taught to apply various problem-solving strategies by engaging in positive self-talk (e.g., telling themselves, "I know how to get out of this argument without having to use my fists,") or self-cueing (e.g., recognizing that their jaws are clenched, they are getting upset, and they need to ask to be excused). Students also are taught to do the following:

- *Self-monitor.* Count the frequency or duration of their own behavior.
- *Self-evaluate.* Compare the change in their behavior to a certain standard to determine whether they are making progress or not.
- *Self-reinforce.* Give themselves rewards when their behavior has reached certain criteria.

For example, Gloria may be taught to count and record the number of times she appropriately raises her hand and waits to be called on during class discussion. She can then determine whether she has met the daily criteria of at least three hand-raises. She then can look at her record of hand-raises for the week, determine if she is making progress toward her goal or not, and collect points to use at the class store later in the week.

Some interventions should be implemented indefinitely, while others will eventually need to stop. For example, Julio is learning to use social problem-solving skills instead of getting into fights on the playground (an intervention that we hope Julio will use forever). He is learning to ask for adult support when he feels like he might get into a fight, and his team has decided that he can earn points for the class token economy when he seeks help appropriately rather than fighting (an intervention that must end at some point). Knowing that he cannot get points for the rest of his life, the team has decided to use the technique of fading once Julio has reached a certain criterion; that is, Julio's teachers will gradually decrease the use of points or other tangible rewards.

This could be done in several ways. First, his teacher could increase the amount of time Julio has to remain "fight-free" to receive a reward. For example, he may initially receive rewards daily, but as he reaches criterion, the time between rewards could be increased to every other day, then once a week, and so on. Another way to fade the intervention is for his teacher to award him fewer points until he is receiving no points at all. For instance, Julio could initially earn 50 points per day for not fighting. This could be reduced to 40, then 30, and so on. It is very important to note that the social reinforcement should continue and eventually replace the tangible rewards. If this process is gradual and Julio is helped to realize the advantages of using appropriate social problem solving, remaining fight-free will become intrinsically rewarding to him.

The success of these strategies may depend on providing the student with periodic "booster" training to review the instruction used in the original intervention plan. Some students also may need to receive self-advocacy training to teach them how to ask for positive recognition or call attention to positive changes in their behavior appropriately. This is especially important for students who have such bad reputations that adults and peers do not recognize when their behaviors are changing. Finally, school personnel can support changes in student performance by accepting "barely noticeable differences," incremental changes that reflect the fact the student is taking positive steps toward the desired goal.

Whole-Classroom Instructional Strategies

Following are suggestions for several programming elements that facilitate positive behavior. This material is not intended to be exhaustive; rather, elements are representative of preventive and early intervention strategies.

Expand and Develop Appropriate Social Interactions

Build on social interactions between staff members and each student, including the student with challenging behaviors. Demonstrating positive regard for the student beyond the current behavior will help the child to feel a part of the group. Give additional attention when the student shows interest in a topic or attempts to engage staff appropriately. When the student goes off-task, steer the child toward more appropriate activities through redirection. Do not feed into inappropriate attention seeking by overreacting to disruptive behaviors; such behaviors are probably reinforced by adult interest, negativity, and concern.

Facilitate Appropriate Peer Interaction

Use group activities to build positive social interaction among students. Teach appropriate social language, how to interact reciprocally, and strategies for getting attention from others and for getting needs met. Teach appropriate language for social interactions during board games, recess activities, snack time, or group discussions. Provide opportunities for cooperative learning.

Review and Rehearse Daily Schedule

Students with significant memory impairments, some learning disabilities, emotional disturbances, autism, or mental retardation are frequently anxious during change or transition. They adapt very well to consistent scheduling and routine. Eventually, they learn most of the routines and can be very resistant to change. This internalization of routine is a means of control, and a student can become quite agitated, act silly, or be disruptive when experiencing unexpected change.

One means for compensating for this problem and building in functional academic experience is verbal rehearsal of scheduling. At the start of the day, go over the sequence of classroom activities verbally and pictorially, if possible. The pictures, icons, logos, and line drawings should be kept with the student for continuous reference. Sequence, not time, should be the emphasis of these rehearsals, but as an incidental training activity, the time of a particular activity also could be displayed beside it. This technique is a concrete and functional approach to reading and time-telling. In addition, it helps to relieve any anxiety associated with change and transition within a hectic or busy environment. This schedule can become a crutch when adult attention at transition time is not available, and it can be used in preparing the student for change on any given day. Knowing how long they have to wait for playtime or free time is important for many students. Coordinate the use of the schedule with other staff members working with the student so that information on the schedule will be accurate. Do not schedule and rehearse events that cannot be delivered reliably. The schedules can allow the student greater awareness, but if not followed consistently, they will irritate rather than reassure the student.

Review and Rehearse Classroom Rules

Actively teach easily generalized, specific rules. Rule teaching is a primary strategy for students with difficulties in concept formation and generalization. Rules should be stated as positive behaviors, such as "hands and feet to self" rather than "no hitting." They may have to be shown to the student in a very concrete fashion, and they may need to be stated before the student begins work. For example, before beginning the lesson, the teacher might show the student a picture of the student or a classmate working appropriately. The teacher would state, "The rule is you must work quietly." The student would then be asked to repeat the rule, and the student would be reinforced for following that rule.

Initially, only one to two rules should be taught at a time. It is important that the student internalize each rule in turn before others are taught contingently. The student may not always succeed in observing the rule, but the teacher must be consistent in expectations. Reminders of the rule should be given whenever the student does not follow it. Initially, all work should be evaluated by the student's ability to follow the rules while working. Quality and quantity of work are not the issue at this time. As the student acquires rules-driven classroom behavior and exhibits an interest in school work, quality and quantity can be re-evaluated. Also, rehearse appropriate rules and strategies before activities begin that may be difficult for the student.

Use Schedules Within Activities to Enhance Structures

It is equally important to structure tasks clearly and concretely when asking the student to work independently. Making the student aware of behavioral expectations, task sequence, and duration may be necessary to support focusing on the activity without distraction, undue anxiety, or disruptive and demanding behavior. The use of written or pictorial schedules may be of use here. Schedules can be used situationally to show the order of events within an activity, as in this example:

1. Use your name stamp on this paper.

2. Circle what you need for this activity.

3. Hand in your work.

Pictures or line drawings are available through many educational resources, especially through speech and language service providers or in critical/functional skills curricula. If the student can read, then short, simple sentences will suffice, along with pictures to enhance communication when possible and desirable.

Teach Coping Skills

This strategy can be especially effective when students are having difficulty following rules. Teach rules in motivating settings and during motivating activities. When a student is involved in motivating activities, remind him or her of the rules for appropriate behavior. Have the student occasionally state the rule when in danger of not following it. When the student is not involved in motivating activities or when activities become too stimulating or anxiety producing, teach the student to state a need to escape; for example, "It's too hard!" or "I need to leave!" or "I need help!" Any verbal explanation that allows the student to escape in an appropriate manner will do. When the student is aware of appropriate options for escaping difficult tasks or for reducing sensory stimuli, then it will be possible to negotiate with a rule, such as, "Try your best!" If the student is agitated or upset, teaching the child to use a relaxation area, such as a corner with a mat or pillows, may be a helpful additional coping strategy if consistently used.

Focus on Whole-Class Positive Behavior

Use the end of the class to comment on positive achievement of all class members. Allow all students to comment on good things they saw others doing. Build a classroom spirit around following classroom rules. Use stickers, praise, applause, additional playtime, or edibles as appropriate when doing this group activity.

Select and Teach Replacement Behaviors

1. *What are replacement behaviors?* In addition to manipulating the environment and integrating whole-classroom positive strategies, a positive approach to behavioral intervention teaches students replacement behaviors that will be as effective in meeting their needs as their challenging behaviors have been. Here are some examples:

- Allison learns to ask for a hug from her teachers and peers instead of roughhousing with them whenever she needs attention.
- Joseph learns to take a pass from the teacher's desk and go visit another adult (principal, nurse, janitor) whenever he

feels anxious. The pass is signed by his teacher and the other supportive adult to ensure accountability.

- Malcolm learns to ask for help from a peer partner when he feels he can't do a problem, instead of swearing or shouting.

2. *Guidelines for selecting replacement behaviors.* Replacement behaviors should always be selected with student, family, and educator input and practiced with all people involved. Students engage in challenging behaviors to meet specific needs. When selecting replacement behaviors, the team should address the following questions. Will the replacement behavior

- work as well as the challenging behavior in meeting the student's needs?
- be an acceptable alternative to the challenging behavior?
- be something that the student chooses to do and that is supported by family and teachers?
- help build a positive reputation for the student?

A replacement behavior can be a new behavior or a behavior the student already performs but not on a regular basis. For example, Allison knows how to ask for a hug, but she does not ask for one consistently. By encouraging and rewarding Allison to ask for a hug, Allison's teachers are able to teach an acceptable alternative to hitting. Joseph, on the other hand, is introduced to a new way of coping: he is taught to pick up a pass from the teacher's desk and leave the room when he feels anxious.

3. *Strategies for teaching replacement behavior.* There are a number of strategies for teaching replacement behavior. Once the team chooses a replacement behavior, consider the following tips and ideas for teaching it:

- Identify what the student has learned during the past year and find out what teaching strategies and assistance were most effective.
- In the beginning, practice the new behavior when the student is calm and relaxed and when problems are not occurring.
- Provide multiple opportunities for the student to role-play and practice using the new behavior (e.g., in different classes, recess, home).
- In addition to teaching the student *how* to perform the new behavior, teach *when* to use it.
- To teach the student to self-initiate performing the skill, use such procedures as role-playing and practice with feedback

in the natural environment. Teach the student to recognize the specific situational and internal cues (e.g., the student's heart is pounding just before it is time to read aloud) that naturally happen before the behavior should occur. Overall, minimize the use of teacher-related cues because they foster dependency on the teacher.

- Try to anticipate when the student is about to make a mistake (experience difficulty when initially learning a new coping skill) and provide support to ensure success, but make sure to allow enough time for the student to self-initiate participation. Ask what the student wants you to *do* (nonverbal cues) or *say* (verbal cues) to cue him or her to practice the new skill.

- Recognize that we all need different levels of support at different times. Be willing to increase or decrease the level of support based on the moment-to-moment needs of the student.

Step III

Become Culturally Competent When Working With Students With Emotional and/or Behavioral Disorders

Most of us have had the humbling experience of realizing that a judgment we made about a person or a situation was inaccurate because we "didn't have all the facts." When considering a challenging behavior exhibited by a student, we must consider some critical facts that have to do with the student's cultural background.

Misperceptions and conflicts frequently arise between teachers and students—and between students and peers—when cultural differences are disregarded. Stereotypes are also reinforced on both sides.

Consider the following examples:

- A student from an Asian background may appear to the teacher as withdrawn while, in the student's cultural context, the child is doing exactly what students are supposed to be doing—listening quietly and respectfully to the teacher. In the family's culture, teachers are the imparters of wisdom, and students are to absorb, not question the teacher.

- Children of color frequently are labeled disruptive for behavior that is not considered disruptive in their cultures. For instance, African American students may have learned in their culture to act assertively. In response to a teacher's request, the student may answer, "No," which the teacher may perceive as rebellious and noncompliant behavior. In reality, the student may have left unspoken a portion of the meaning of the response, that "No" carries the implicit " . . . unless I can see the importance of the task or request."

- A teacher, addressing a student who belongs to a Native American tribe, may become annoyed when the student will not look at him or her and may interpret the behavior as inattentive, rude, disrespectful, disinterested, and/or hostile. However, the student may come from a culture where it is disrespectful for a child to have eye contact with an adult.

- In another situation, a teacher may judge a student who is a member of a Native American tribe to be "withdrawn" and "sullen" because the child doesn't participate in class discussions or respond to questions that the teacher knows the student is able to answer. The student, however, may be neither sullen nor withdrawn. Rather, the student may not want classmates to be shamed because they don't know the answer.

- In Hispanic language, objects may be lost without having to say "who" lost the object. In the English language, someone is usually responsible for the action. So if a teacher comes up to a student and says, "Maria, where is your book?" and Maria says, "The book got lost," the teacher may feel it important to emphasize, "Maria, *you* lost the book. It didn't get lost by itself." Maria may be confused between English at school and Spanish at home and be trying to manage two sets of values.

- Latino culture generally stresses interdependence far more than does American culture of Northern European heritage. Those regarded as *family* may include extended family: aunts, uncles, grandparents, cousins, etc. In addition, a strong kinship bond often exists between children and their godparents that lasts from birth to death. For students from such backgrounds in particular, an all-business approach by a teacher may seem cold and uncaring. A teacher wishing to collaborate with such a student in problem solving would do well to begin by asking about the student's family in a genuinely interested manner. Otherwise, the most the teacher might receive from the student may be yes or no.

- For many cultures, the honor of the family is the primary value and a powerful motivational force. A child may, in fact, lie to save face for the family. Imposing consequences for lying without understanding what is at stake for the child in telling the truth may lead to approaches that can alienate the student.
- Some persons of Asian descent feel a sense of stigmatization around mental illness—though obviously such a view is not limited to Asian cultures. Therefore, when an Asian American student suspected of an emotional or behavioral disorder is undergoing assessment, some information the student or family member gives may be altered so as to protect the assumed origin (e.g., family lineage, demonic spirits) of a particularly disturbing behavior. Altered information may also be provided if there is suspicion by the family regarding the use of that information by the mental health or school professional. Confidentiality may have been abused in the family's past history, particularly by the government or other officials in the family's native land (Ishii-Jordan & Peterson, 1994),
- Children who have moved to the United States from other countries or even from other parts of the United States may have left traumatic situations. Children who have lived amidst warfare and minefields, or whose families have sought the relative safety of the United States after being victimized by crime elsewhere, may be suffering from posttraumatic stress disorder. Children whose parents lived through traumatic events may experience "secondary trauma," even though they themselves were born in the United States. Their parents may be so affected by the past that they are unable to provide the kind of nurturing and discipline that their children need.
- Other students who have grown up in difficult circumstances may have learned behaviors that are maladaptive in America. For example, some students grew up in orphanages, on the streets, or in places where food is scarce. Children who have had to wait in long lines for food may push and shove to get to the front of cafeteria lines. This is a survival skill that was necessary in their previous environment; they need help in learning that it is no longer necessary.
- Many students are in transition from one culture to another. They may wish to act like their American-born peers but do not understand the boundaries of acceptable behavior. The children's desire to become acculturated can also cause stress in families when parents and grandparents maintain traditional values and expect traditional behavior.

Recognizing that within ethnic and racial designations, considerable variation exists in language, history, values, religion, and understanding of "family," the situations described above are examples only and should not be understood as "typical" ways of responding by all students or families from a given cultural background. They are presented as reminders of the importance of becoming "culturally literate." This skill is particularly important when addressing behavior that is challenging. Peterson and Ishii-Jordan (1994) point out that:

> to treat . . ."maladaptive" behavior, we must . . . understand the way a particular culture or community views that behavior and its own strategies for "treating" or "changing" that behavior. In some cultures deviant behavior is viewed as requiring "religious" or "spiritual" intervention, whereas western cultures tend to rely on "positivist scientific" explanations and interventions. (pp. 11–12)

Some Tips

- As educators, we should refrain from making assumptions about cultures and traditions that we do not fully understand.
- Interview the child (or do group work with students), getting *that child's* perspective on the behavior and its purpose/meaning. Be genuinely and gratefully willing to learn from students. Give them information about the effects of their behavior in the school setting, while showing understanding and respect for their cultures.
- Look at specific learning styles, because many are based upon cultural differences. How can these styles be supported?
- If a student has just transferred to a district, find out where he or she was previously enrolled. Behavioral norms may vary from district to district, and these differences may explain a student's behavioral repertoire and provide insight into instructional strategies.

Note that in some cultures,

> if personal information is desired, the [direct] asking for information may be looked upon as a breach of etiquette. Often, more information will be forthcoming if a somewhat circuitous route is taken. Instead of asking a direct question, if the professional will first share information about his/her

family, home, etc., the student and/or his/her family might then begin to develop the trust necessary to share the desired information. In all things, patience is the key to success. (Kallam, Hoernicke, & Coser, 1994, p. 135)

Include the parents and any extended family or community member who may be particularly significant in the student's life. When interviewing, be warm and inviting. Learn from them. Asking, "Is the father involved?" may be very insulting. In some cultures, extended family members are as important as parents in the life of the child. We cannot assume that a difference in last names means that children have different fathers or that their parents are not married. For example, taking a name in honor of someone special in their lives is common for persons in Native American cultures.

Step IV

Understand and Apply Principles of Reinforcement When Working With Students With Emotional and/or Behavioral Disorders

One of the most common errors in classroom management for children with emotional and/or behavioral disorders relates to a confusion between reward and reinforcement. *Reinforcement* is said to have occurred when a consequence to a behavior results in that behavior's increasing or maintaining in frequency. Thus, the behavior is reinforced—made stronger and more resistant to elimination—because the individual desires the reinforcer and associates the behavior with desirable outcomes. A *reward*, on the other hand, is given by an observer for having met some criterion established by the observer. Frequently, the giver assumes the recipient will like the outcome, but the receiver may actually dislike the reward. A reward is what you think will work; a reinforcer is what is proven to work.

What Is the Actual Reinforcer?

It is important to determine which elements in each reinforcement act are actually reinforcing. For example, if the student is responsive to stickers or other tangibles given by the teacher, is the reinforcer successful because of

- love of the object itself?
- the "closure" element of filling every square on the sheet?
- the student's sense of success and positive feelings about self following internal self-talk praising the accomplishment?
- love of getting something peers are not getting?
- the desire for touch, which is satisfied when the teacher pats the student on the back when giving the sticker?
- some other feature?

It is easier to design effective strategies to increase positive behaviors if one understands as precisely as possible what element is reinforcing to the individual. Activities and interests that the student actively pursues are good areas to explore. Interviews with the individual and significant others, as well as observation during the functional analysis, will frequently yield important information as to what reinforces student behavior. Many published reinforcer surveys can be helpful in this process.

Factors Affecting Reinforcer Effectiveness

For greatest effectiveness, reinforcers should

- be selected for a behavior that the student can proficiently perform or for which instruction will be provided (often including shaping or modeling techniques);
- have enough power to affect the specific behavior;
- include sufficient variability to maintain effectiveness in the program;
- meet the student's immediacy needs; and
- meet the student's frequency needs.

Checklist for Effective Reinforcement

Measurement

- Check to be sure the measurements of the effect of the reinforcer on behavior are correct.

Instruction

- Select behaviors that can be maintained by the natural environment over time; plan for and teach skills necessary for generalization and maintenance.
- Reinforce closer and closer approximation to the goal behavior (shaping behavior); effectively prompt or cue the student to perform the behavior to gain the reinforcer as necessary.
- The positive alternative behavior should be taught in small steps. Expecting a fully proficient skill to be learned without task analysis and instruction can lead to failure. Make sure the targeted replacement behaviors and approximations are possible.
- Avoid giving prompts too often during the teaching process to prevent the student from becoming prompt-dependent. For example, give the student a signal only when attention should be directed to the instructor. Give the signal only once. Wait a few seconds. Then either (a) let the student find out that the consequence of failing to perform the behavior is missing the reinforcer or (b) give the signal again and prompt the student through the motions of the desired behavior.
- Never use threats as signals; they are not positive teaching tools.

Frequency

- Give the reinforcer frequently enough to support the behavior (i.e., avoid requiring too many responses before reinforcement). Consider the developmental level in program design. At the start of any program to change behavior, it is very important that the behavior be rewarded nearly every time it happens; that is, on a continuous schedule.
- Make the shift from a continuous schedule to an intermittent schedule *gradually*. For example, it is best, when shifting from a continuous schedule, to reward the behavior every time, then four out of five times, then two out of three, and so forth.
- Ask, "Is the student continuing to be rewarded every so often for behaviors that were heavily reinforced in the past?" Intermittent reinforcement helps make a behavior resistant to extinction.

Immediacy

- Avoid a lengthy (by the student's standards) delay in accessing the reinforcer. Immediacy problems can be a result of reduced ability to delay gratification because of a variety of factors, such as developmental level, emotional disturbance, or lack of experience in receiving reinforcers.

- If some delay is necessary and the student requires an immediate reinforcer (e.g., food or a token), giving the student some signal that the reinforcer is forthcoming can be effective until the teacher is able to give it. When consequences are not given fast enough, the student may fail to recognize what is being reinforced. The behavior just before the reinforcer may be the one that is reinforced and, therefore, be the behavior that will likely increase.

Power and Variety

- Select reinforcers that are powerful enough to replace the reinforcer currently present following the challenging behavior.
- Be certain that the so-called reinforcer is really desirable to the individual (e.g., through use of a reinforcement inventory). It is important always to check the effectiveness of the consequence on the behavior.
- Offer enough variety and complexity. Satiation occurs when a student receives the same reinforcer so many times that it is not a reward any more. Switching between many different kinds of reinforcers may be effective. Stop an activity before the child has had enough. As soon as a child shows signs of becoming satiated on a reinforcer, limit its use.
- Be aware of whether the student is getting other reinforcers (e.g., attention) for free. If the student already gets a form of whatever the teacher is going to provide, the reinforcer may not have sufficient power to effect change (Wright & Gurman, 1994).

Possible Reinforcers

The following list of reinforcers offers possibilities from which to brainstorm other ideas using resources available in your students' environments. In addition, observe to see what a student chooses during free time. It is important to remember that some students may find a reinforcer listed here highly aversive rather than reinforcing. Developmental level, chronological age, and personal likes and dislikes must always be considered in selecting potential reinforcers; validate a reinforcer by discussing it with the student, caregivers, or others with knowledge of the student. Immediacy, frequency, power, and variability needs of the student must be considered equally in selecting reinforcers.

Commonly Available Reinforcers

- Cafeteria helper at the lunch counter
- Chance to help others
- Choose a game; be teacher for the day
- Class leader to bathroom
- Class leader to cafeteria
- Class proctor
- Clean chalk board
- Computer time
- Crosswalk patrol leader
- Daily, weekly, and monthly good reports to parents
- Extra privileges
- Feed classroom animals
- Field trips
- First turn
- Flag raiser
- Game equipment manager
- Get to sit by a friend
- Go to locker one minute early
- Happy faces on paper
- Library passes
- Library time
- Listen to records
- Lunch with teacher or principal
- Magazine selection
- Messenger
- Model building
- Music pass
- Nurse's helper
- Papers on wall
- Party after school
- Pat on back by teacher
- Picnic
- Praise
- Read to younger children
- Roll call leader
- Self-graphing
- Self-selection of activity
- Sharpen pencils for class
- Sit by door
- Sit by windows
- Sit in back of classroom

- Sit in front of classroom
- Smiles of teacher
- Stamps on hand
- Stars on paper
- Turn lights off and on

Home Reinforcers

Note that the teacher may find these useful in developing plans involving multiple environments.

- Buy something for the car
- Candy
- Choose a gift for a friend or sibling
- Choose a particular food
- Choose a TV program
- Choose own clothing to wear
- Choose own hairstyle
- Coloring carbons
- Entertain friends
- Extra helping at dinner
- Extra playtime
- Extra time at TV
- Extra time before going to bed
- Fewer chores
- Friend to spend the night
- Go on errands
- Go out to a special restaurant
- Go to a movie
- Go to a summer camp
- Go to the zoo
- Gum
- Have a friend over
- Have a picnic
- Have breakfast in bed
- Help make a dog house
- Increase allowance
- Lick stamps or stickers
- Make something for the teacher
- Make something in the kitchen
- Money
- New clothes
- New toys

- Not have to iron own clothes for a week
- Not have to wash clothes for a week
- Open the mail
- Opportunity to go out for sports at school
- Parties
- Pat on back
- Piggyback ride on dad
- Play a game with parents
- Praise
- Records
- Select computer/video/handheld game
- Sleep later on weekends
- Soda
- Start a fire in fireplace
- Swimming
- Take pictures of friends
- Time outside
- Use adult tools
- Wash and dry dishes
- Watch dad shave
- Watch more TV shows
- Work to go to the circus
- Wrap gifts

Individual Activities and Privileges

- Answer questions
- Assist the teacher to teach
- Best Kid of the Day
- Care for class pets, flowers, etc.
- Choose activities
- Classroom supervision
- Collect materials—papers, workbooks, assignments, etc.
- Construct school materials
- Correct papers
- Decorate room
- Display student's work
- Dust, erase, clean
- First in line
- Help with outside activities (e.g., patrols, represent group in school activities directing parking, ushering, etc.)
- Lead discussion
- Lead student groups

- Make gifts
- Put away materials
- Read a story
- Recognize birthdays
- Responsibility for ongoing activities
- Run errands
- Show and tell—any level
- Special seating arrangements
- Straighten up for teacher
- Work problems on the board

Social Reinforcers for Individuals or Groups

- Compete with other classes
- Dance
- Decorate classroom
- Field trips
- Go to museum, fire station, courthouse, etc.
- Make subject-matter games
- Movies
- Musical chairs
- Participate in group organizations
- Parties
- Perform for PTA
- Picnics
- Plan daily schedules
- Play records
- Prepare for holidays
- Present skits
- Puppet shows
- Recess or play periods
- Talent shows (joking, reading, music)
- Talking periods
- Visit another class

Reinforcement of Appropriate Student Behavior

When trying to determine the best reinforcer to use for each student in your classroom, knowledge of student preferences and strengths is useful. We might ask what types of things a student likes (e.g., time on the computer, being allowed to run errands), watch for and record any preferred activities, or use an informal survey of reinforcement preferences (i.e., forced-choice reinforcement menu). It is important to be consistent in the frequency of the delivery of the reinforcer, but it is also good to vary the actual reinforcers routinely, so that the student does not tire or become bored with a particular reinforcer. When developing a plan, it is also important to consider the amount of reinforcement in relationship to the amount of student effort to obtain it. In some cases, it may be necessary initially to offer a student "noncontingent" access to a reinforcer (e.g., with "no strings attached"), especially if the reinforcer is something the student has never had. Called "reinforcer sampling," this is one way to let the student know that the thing or activity is reinforcing. For example, we might allow a student to participate in a highly preferred activity with a classmate (e.g., a computer-based learning activity). If the student enjoys it, access to that activity would later depend on the student's engaging in the desired appropriate behavior.

Sometimes, the desired response may call for too dramatic a change in the student's behavior (i.e., a change the student is unable and/or unwilling to make all at once). If that is the case, you will need to accept successive approximations or gradual changes toward the desired behavior. For example, Tyrone may not be able to handle the pressure that stems from a highly complex academic assignment, particularly when he has had too little sleep. A first step might be to teach Tyrone to ask politely to be temporarily excused from a particular activity (i.e., replacement behavior that achieves the same outcome as the problem behavior). However, the long-term plan would be for Tyrone to develop increased self-control, to master and complete complex academic assignments, and to solicit peer support (i.e., desired behaviors). Attempts also should be made to encourage the family to find ways for Tyrone to get more sleep.

A final consideration in using reinforcers is the process of fading, or gradually replacing extrinsic rewards with more natural or intrinsic rewards on a realistic or natural time schedule. Of course, fading will only be a consideration once the student has shown an increased ability and willingness to engage in the appropriate, desired behavior. The process of fading may be made easier by pairing the extrinsic reward with an intrinsic reward. For example, when rewarding Danielle with points for completing a homework assignment, the paraprofessional could also say, "Danielle, you've finished all your homework this week, and your class participation has increased because you are better prepared. You must be very proud of yourself for the hard work you have done."

Step V

Promote Positive Social Interactions Among Students With Emotional and/or Behavioral Disorders

The feeling of belonging positively affects a student's self-image and self-esteem, motivation to achieve, speed of adjustment to the larger classroom and new demands, general behavior, and general level of achievement. The impact of a new student on the general classroom is a major consideration for teachers. Fostering positive social relationships between students with disabilities and their peers requires the preparation of nondisabled peers so that they understand the needs of their new classmates. Teachers may use many strategies to help the new student achieve a sense of belonging to the class and school.

One of the most critical things a classroom teacher must do is establish and maintain a positive and supportive classroom atmosphere. Students are more likely to follow directions, work hard, and exhibit positive classroom behavior when they feel wanted and appreciated by the teacher. This may be especially true of particularly difficult students, who may not trust adults and who may feel that most teachers are "out to get them."

Why Are Social Skills Important?

Social competence is the degree to which students are able to establish and maintain satisfactory interpersonal relationships, gain peer acceptance, establish and maintain friendships, and terminate negative or pernicious interpersonal relationships. Effective social problem solving requires reading one's own and others' feelings and being able to label and express those feelings accurately. Such skills are aspects of social and emotional learning (Zins et al., 1998, p. 19). Well-developed social skills can help youth with disabilities develop strong and positive peer relationships, succeed in school, and begin successfully to explore adult roles such as employee, coworker/colleague, and community member. Social skills also support the positive development of healthy adult relationships with family members and peers. Hair, Jager, and Garrett (2002) observe that adolescents who have strong social skills, particularly in the areas of conflict resolution, emotional intimacy, and the use of pro-social behaviors, are more likely to be accepted by peers, develop friendships, maintain stronger relationships with parents and peers, be viewed as effective problem solvers, cultivate greater interest in school, and perform better academically (p. 3). Adequate social skills need to be acquired while students are still enrolled in school and further supported and refined in postsecondary, community, and work settings.

Social-Cognitive Skill Development

Social relationships are an important aspect of the learning process and the classroom environment. Research has demonstrated that a significant proportion of students who fail to adjust socially to the classroom environment lack effective social problem-solving skills. Social problems include the following:

- Poor ability to be empathetic to others' perspectives
- Poor impulse control
- Inability to generate multiple and effective solutions to problems faced in the classroom

Deficiencies in cognitive problem-solving skills often lead to emotional and behavioral disorders requiring treatment. The teacher in the inclusive classroom needs to address the social-behavioral domain as well as the academic domain. Research on teaching indicates giving training in social-cognitive skills to youth who are at risk of failure in general education classrooms can improve student's social effectiveness, help the student to achieve social goals, and reduce problem behaviors (Kochhar, West, & Taymans, 2000).

The Role of Social Skills at School

Gresham, Sugai, and Horner (2001) note that deficits in social skills are key criteria in defining many high-incidence disabilities that hinder students' academic progress, such as specific learning disabilities, attention deficit/hyperactivity disorder (ADHD), mental retardation, and emotional disturbance (p. 332). Therefore, helping students learn social skills is a proactive approach to minimizing the impact of these types of disabilities on school success.

When social skills are absent, educators cannot fully engage students in a variety of learning experiences, especially those that are cooperative. As classroom teachers increasingly use cooperative learning strategies across their curricula, the need for students to have strong social skills is evident. To participate fully in cooperative learning, some students with disabilities need training in skills such as giving and receiving feedback, listening, and appropriate self-disclosure.

Strategies to Foster a Sense of Belonging in the Classroom

Any teacher who has tried to improve a student's social skills knows that such an endeavor presents significant challenges. Problems that interfere with the effectiveness of social skill interventions may include oppositional behavior, conduct problems, negative influences from peer groups, substance abuse, family difficulties, and limited cognitive abilities (Hansen, Nangle, & Meyer, 1998).

Why would students want to improve their social skills? Most likely, they seek to (a) avoid the negative consequences of inadequate social skills, including loneliness, job loss, or embarrassment at school or work and (b) enjoy the benefits of having good social skills, such as friendship, acceptance from others, and good relationships at school and work. Nonetheless, students must see the need for the skills being taught. In the classroom, teachers may ask students to identify the social skills necessary for achieving goals important to them. Based on such discussions, students and teachers can jointly select one or two skills to work on at a time.

One of the measures of successful of teaching is the degree to which the student with a disability feels a part of the classroom. The feeling of belonging positively affects the student's self-image and self-esteem, motivation to achieve, speed of adjustment to the larger classroom and new demands, general behavior, and general level of achievement. Fostering positive social relationships between students with disabilities and their peers requires the preparation of nondisabled peers in the classroom so that they understand the needs of their new classmates. Teachers may use many strategies to help the student achieve a sense of belonging to the class and school including the following (Kochhar et al., 2000):

- Discuss expectations with the student's peers and encourage interaction; the school counselor or psychologist can be helpful in preparing classes for a new student with a disability and in discussing the benefits of positive peer relationships.
- Use cooperative group learning, in which students are teamed for activities or projects and must cooperate, share ideas and materials, and share in the development of project products. Learning teams are also effective when students are required to prepare for classroom demonstrations and exhibitions.
- Assign peer advocates, a peer mentor, or a "buddy" who is responsible for interacting with and helping the student in classroom activities and social situations. The peer advocate provides support and encouragement and enables the student with a disability to solve problems with class activities and generally adjust to the new classroom environment.
- Assign a teacher advocate to the student whom the student can consult for guidance, general support, or crisis assistance.
- Include the new student in the daily roll call and in all class pictures and place the student's work on the bulletin boards right along with the work of peers.
- Establish a lunch-buddy system (particularly helpful for younger students in the first weeks of class).

Creating a Positive Classroom Climate

Consistent and effective use of acquired social skills is more likely to occur in classrooms having a positive social atmosphere. Most adults can think of a situation in which they didn't feel valued and, as a result, did not respond appropriately or compassionately to others. The classroom can ensure that all students know they are valued and respected members of a learning community by taking the following steps to create a positive school climate (Curtis, 2003):

- Learn and use students' names and know something about each student. This can be difficult in secondary schools; using name tags or assigned seating at the beginning of each term can be helpful.
- Hold daily classroom meetings each morning to help build a sense of community and provide opportunities for conversation among students.
- Provide unstructured time (e.g., recess) when students can practice their social skills with peers and experience feedback.
- Encourage journal writing to improve self-awareness.
- Provide opportunities for students to participate noncompetitively (without tryouts or auditions) in extracurricular activities. Avoid unnecessary competition among students.
- Provide ways for students to provide feedback regarding their experience at school and show them that their input is taken seriously.
- Make a point of connecting briefly and informally, over a period of several days, with individual students who are having difficulties. This communication establishes a relationship that will be helpful if the student's situation requires a more formal discussion at another time.

To be effective and worthwhile, social skills training must result in skills that (a) are socially relevant in the individual's life (social validity), (b) are used in a variety of situations (generalization), and (c) are maintained over time (treatment adherence) (Hansen et al., 1998). Such skills will be most consistently employed in a setting that is supportive and respectful of each person's individuality.

Teaching Social Skills Through Role-Playing and Observation

Role-playing is a helpful technique for engaging student interest and providing opportunities for practice and feedback. One way to establish motivation and to inject some humor into the learning process is to ask students to role-play a situation in which the identified skill is lacking. Role-playing allows students to take on roles, provide feedback to one another, and practice new skills. Role-playing enables students to simulate a wide range of school, community, and workplace interactions. For students with intellectual disabilities, role-playing can provide an opportunity to practice appropriate small talk, a social skill that is key to acceptance in the classroom.

Role-playing exercises can help develop automaticity with small talk appropriate to the classroom. They include the following:

- Practicing automatic and brief responses for greetings and farewells. Responses should be brief, appropriate, and unelaborated. To "how" questions (e.g., "How are you doing?") an appropriate response is "Fine" or "Great." To "what" questions (e.g., "What's up?"), an appropriate response is "Not much." The ability to use automatic and appropriate responses can be helpful in getting off to a good start in a new classroom or workplace.
- Practicing extending small talk by learning to add questions like "How about you?" or "What about you?" or "What have you been doing?" to the above responses.
- Role-playing an interaction that includes acting out social errors, spotting the errors, and correcting them in a subsequent role-play (with more able young adults). Examples of errors include bringing up inappropriate topics for small talk, giving an inappropriately long response or no response when one is needed, giving an inappropriately detailed response, and using a small-talk formula when it is not appropriate.

The Classroom Teacher's Power to Model Acceptance

Many schools are establishing peer-mentor relationships to educate nondisabled peers and help build relationships for emotional and social support. However, probably the most important influence on positive classroom relationships and social attitudes is the attitude of the teacher and the degree to which the teacher models acceptance of students with special needs. Classroom teachers must directly address the importance of mutual acceptance and support within the classroom, and they must reflect on their own attitudes and ability to demonstrate such acceptance (Kochhar et al., 2000).

Promoting Positive Social Interactions Among Students With and Without Disabilities

Effective classroom teachers are distinguished by their positive approach to dealing with disciplinary problems. Rather than waiting for problems to develop and then reacting, effective classroom teachers organize their classrooms to promote positive behavior. Rather than looking for a quick fix for behavioral problems and issues, effective classroom teachers make a commitment to long-term behavioral change. This section will focus on strategies to promote positive social interactions among all students, which effective classroom teachers can use in their everyday teaching and daily routine both in and outside of the classroom.

Conduct Class Meetings

During class meetings, students, as a group, can share their opinions and brainstorm solutions to class behavior problems and general topics that concern students. Class meetings are designed to help students understand the perspectives of others, so they are especially effective for resolving conflicts based on cultural differences. Classroom problems and tensions between students in the classroom can be identified and handled by placing a box in the classroom where students and adults submit both compliments and descriptions of problems and situations that made them feel upset, sad, annoyed, or angry. Compliments and concerns can be shared with the class, and all students can brainstorm possible solutions.

Use Values Clarification

Values clarification views classroom misbehavior as being a result of confused values. Values clarification activities that are part of the curriculum allow students to examine their attitudes, interests, and feelings and learn how these values affect their behavior. For example, after students express their attitudes or opinions or use a specific behavior, you might ask, "How did that affect you and others?" "Why is that important to you?" and "Did you consider any alternatives?" You can also use values clarification by creating a non-judgmental, open, and trusting environment. Such an atmosphere encourages students to share their values, feelings, and beliefs and respect those of others (Salend, 2001).

Use Praise As Often As Possible

Effective teachers use a number of behavioral intervention techniques to help students learn how to manage their behavior. Perhaps the most important and effective of these is verbal reinforcement of appropriate behavior. The most common form of verbal reinforcement is praise given to a student when he begins and completes an activity or exhibits a particular desired behavior. Simple phrases such as "good job" encourage a student to act appropriately. Effective teachers praise students frequently and look for a behavior to praise before, not after, a student gets off-task.

The following strategies provide some guidance regarding the use of praise:

- *Define the appropriate behavior while giving praise.* Praise should be specific for the positive behavior displayed by the student: the comments should focus on what the student did right and should include exactly what part(s) of the student's behavior was desirable. Rather than praising a student for not disturbing the class, for example, a teacher should praise her for quietly completing a math lesson on time.
- *Provide praise immediately.* The sooner that approval is given regarding appropriate behavior, the more likely the student will repeat it.
- *Vary the statements given as praise.* The comments used by teachers to praise appropriate behavior should vary; when students hear the same praise statement repeated over and over, it may lose its value.
- *Be consistent and sincere with praise.* Appropriate behavior should receive consistent praise. Consistency among teachers with respect to desired behavior is important to avoid confusion on the part of students with special needs. Similarly, students will notice when teachers give insincere praise, and this insincerity will make praise less effective.

It is important to keep in mind that the most effective teachers focus their behavioral intervention strategies on *praise* rather than on *punishment*. Negative consequences may temporarily change behavior, but they rarely change attitudes and may actually increase the frequency and intensity of inappropriate behavior by rewarding misbehaving students with attention. Moreover, punishment may only teach students what not to do; it does not provide students with the skills that they need to do what is expected. Positive reinforcement produces the changes in attitudes that will shape a student's behavior over the long term.

Project a Feeling, Caring Persona

Convince students that you like them (even though you might not always like their behaviors). Take time to greet students at the door when they first arrive into the classroom. Address students by name and express an interest in their activities. Build up a store of positive comments to individual students, so that if later you must deliver negative feedback, it is not the first evaluation you have made of the student. Above all, try to assure students that you genuinely like them and that you have their best interests in mind. Even though you will have both positive and negative reactions to their specific behaviors, you nevertheless always value them as individuals.

Use Reprimands Judiciously

Although positive responses to positive behavior are among the best overall methods of classroom management, negative feedback in the form of reprimands is sometimes necessary to help students succeed in your classroom. Overall, reprimands are best viewed as direct feedback that the student's behavior is inappropriate. If they are provided in a way that indicates concern for the student's well-being, they can be effective in improving behavior. Reprimands are less effective when viewed as punishment, when criticism and scorn or a negative, aggressive, or hostile tone of voice are expected to prevent the student from repeating the inappropriate behavior.

Research on reprimands suggests the following (Kerr & Nelson, 2002):

- Reprimand students privately, not publicly, to avoid humiliating or embarrassing them.
- Stand near the student you are reprimanding. This allows you to use a more confidential tone of voice. However, remaining one arm's length away respects the student's personal space.
- Use a normal tone of voice. Students can become desensitized over time to raised voices and may be less inclined to respond defensively to a calm tone.
- Look at the student while you are speaking, but do *not* insist that the student return your eye contact. Forced eye contact can be viewed as hostile and aggressive and, in some cases, can even violate cultural norms.

- Never point your finger at the student you are reprimanding, as this gesture again conveys aggression and hostility.
- Do not insist on having the last word. The final goal of your reprimand is increased compliance with class rules, not in getting in the final word.

Validate Student Feelings

Sometimes when faced with a reprimand, students accuse teachers of unfair treatment. For example, a student might say, "It doesn't matter what I do, you are always picking on me!" This type of accusation often results in a defensive statement from the teacher: "I am not picking on you," or, "I treat everyone in this class the same."

Instead of making a defensive comment, try validating the student's feelings by asking for specifics: "I really don't want you to think I am picking on you. If you give me specific examples, maybe we can solve the problem." Such an approach not only avoids a confrontation, it also validates the student's expressed feeling (whether "true" or not), as well as subtly challenging the student to document "always" being picked on. It also openly attempts to keep the lines of communication open.

Selectively Ignore Inappropriate Behavior

It is sometimes helpful for teachers to ignore inappropriate behavior selectively. This technique is particularly useful when the behavior is unintentional or unlikely to recur or is intended solely to gain the attention of teachers or classmates without disrupting the classroom or interfering with the learning of others.

Provide Activity Reinforcement

Students receive activity reinforcement when they are encouraged to perform a less desirable behavior before a preferred one.

Utilize Peer Mediation

Members of a student's peer group can positively impact the behavior of students with special needs. Many schools now have formalized peer mediation programs in which students receive training to manage disputes involving their classmates.

Use Behavioral Prompts

Effective teachers also use behavioral prompts with their students. These prompts help remind students about expectations for their learning and behavior in the classroom. Three, which may be particularly helpful, are the following:

- *Provide visual cues.* Establish simple, nonintrusive visual cues to remind the student to remain on-task. For example, you can point at the student while looking him or her in the eye, or you can hold out your hand, palm down, near the student.
- *Provide social skills classes.* Teach students with special needs appropriate social skills by using a structured class. For example, you can ask the students to role-play and model different solutions to common social problems. It is critical to provide for the generalization of these skills, including structured opportunities for the students to use the social skills that they learn. Offering such classes, or experiences, to the general school population can positively affect the school climate.
- *Implement problem-solving sessions.* Discuss how to resolve social conflicts. Conduct impromptu discussions with one student or with a small group of students when the conflict arises. For example, ask two students who are arguing about a game to discuss how to settle their differences. Encourage the students to resolve their problem by talking to each other in a supervised setting.

Functional Behavioral Assessments and Positive Behavioral Interventions and Supports

For many students with special needs, functional behavioral assessments and positive behavioral interventions and supports, including behavioral contracts and management plans, tangible rewards, or token economy systems, are helpful in teaching them how to manage their own behavior. Because students' individual needs are different, it is important for teachers, along with the family and other involved professionals, to evaluate whether these practices are appropriate for their classrooms. Examples of these techniques, along with steps to follow when using them, include the following:

- *Establish behavioral contracts and management plans.* Identify specific academic or behavioral goals for the student with special needs, along with behavior that needs to change and strategies for responding to inappropriate behavior. Work with the student cooperatively to identify appropriate goals, such as completing homework assignments on time and obeying safety rules on the school playground. Take the time to ensure that the student agrees that these goals are important to master. Behavioral contracts and management plans are typically used with individual students, as opposed to entire classes, and should be prepared with input from parents.

- *Use tangible rewards.* Use tangible rewards to reinforce appropriate behavior. These rewards can include stickers, such as happy faces or sports team emblems, or privileges, such as extra time on the computer or lunch with the teacher. Students should be involved in the selection of the reward. If students are invested in the reward, they are more likely to work for it.
- *Establish token economy systems.* Use token economy systems to motivate a student to achieve a goal identified in a behavioral contract. For example, a student can earn points for each homework assignment completed on time. In some cases, students also lose points for each homework assignment not completed on time. After earning a specified number of points, the student receives a tangible reward, such as extra time on a computer or a "free" period on Friday afternoon. Token economy systems are often used for entire classrooms, not just for individual students.

Teach Self-Management Systems

Train students to monitor and evaluate their own behavior without constant feedback from the teacher. In a typical self-management system, the teacher identifies behaviors that will be managed by a student and provides a written rating scale that includes the performance criteria for each rating. The teacher and student separately rate student behavior during an activity and compare ratings. The student earns points if the ratings match or are within one point and receives no points if ratings are more than one point apart; points are exchanged for privileges. With time, the teacher involvement is removed, and the student becomes responsible for self-monitoring (DuPaul & Stoner as cited in Shinn, Walker, & Stoner, 2002).

Post Positive Behavior

Public posting of students' behaviors has also been seen to reduce behavior problems. Students' behaviors can be evaluated and recorded on publicly posted charts. Students who follow classroom rules can be given a star next to their name for each class period, day, or other appropriate length of time.

Promote Self-Monitoring

Self-monitoring strategies involve teaching students to monitor and evaluate their own classroom behavior. In some cases, students may be asked to monitor their general on-task behavior. In other cases, students may monitor themselves for a specific behavior, such as teasing. Before implementing self-monitoring interventions, meet individually and discuss with students the purpose and importance of classroom behavior and how they will benefit personally from better classroom behavior. The students should be made to understand that the intervention is in their best interest.

Train for Generalization

Most positive social behaviors are of limited use unless they can be generalized to appropriate situations outside the training context. It is particularly important that students in inclusive settings are able to generalize all the positive social behaviors they have learned in other settings; however, students with special needs often demonstrate problems in generalizing learned behavior. As important social behaviors are learned, make a list of all the settings and situations into which behavior must generalize and all the individuals who will observe the generalized behavior. Then create a plan to promote generalization across all these settings and individuals.

Deal Appropriately With Name-Calling and Teasing

Friendships in classrooms and positive behavior can be established by preventing name-calling and teasing as soon as it happens. Effective behavioral management techniques for these situations include the following:

- Establish a rule about no name-calling and teasing.
- Make it clear to students that name-calling and teasing will not be tolerated.
- Respond immediately to incidents of name-calling and teasing with a discussion of differences and discrimination.
- Help students recognize and explore the reasons why they are uncomfortable with individual differences.
- Help students to understand individual differences by giving them information.

Offer Choices and Solicit Preferences

Allowing students to make choices and express their preferences can promote self-determination. Because the school day involves a series of choices, you can integrate activities involving choices into both teaching and nonteaching parts of the daily schedule. If students have difficulty making choices, you can start by providing them with options. Cooperative learning arrangements, student-selected projects and rewards, self-management and metacognitive techniques, and learning strategies also allow students to guide their own learning.

Promote Self-Esteem

Promoting self-esteem in students can improve their ability to advocate for themselves. Students with low self-esteem often make negative statements about themselves that hinder their performance, such as "I'm not good at this and I'll never complete it." You can promote self-esteem by helping students understand the harmful effects of low self-esteem and by structuring academic and social situations so that students succeed. Other methods include recognizing students' achievements and talents, teaching them to use self-management techniques, asking them to perform meaningful classroom and school-based jobs, and posting their work in the classroom and throughout the school.

Provide Attribution Training

Students' self-determination and self-esteem can be fostered by attribution training, which involves teaching students to analyze the events and actions that lead to success and failure. Students who understand attribution recognize and acknowledge that their positive performance is due to effort and other factors within themselves. Students who fail to understand attribution often attribute their poor performance to bad luck, teacher error, lack of ability, or other external factors.

Demonstrate or Model Rules and Procedures and Allow Students to Rehearse Them

The teacher demonstrates both the correct and incorrect forms of the behavior (e.g., sitting at a desk quietly, going to the pencil sharpener). The demonstration enables the students to discriminate the dimensions of the behavior. Students are then given an opportunity to practice the required behavior. Mastering rules and procedures is similar to learning academics; it requires teacher instruction and feed-back combined with student practice.

After negative attention, provide immediate reinforcement and attention when the student displays the appropriate behavior. This identifies the accepted behavior and reaffirms that appropriate behaviors are reinforced and inappropriate behaviors are punished.

With Older Students, Use Contingency Contracts

Contingency contracts are written agreements between the teacher and the student that indicate what the student must do to earn a specific reward. These agreements, like most contracts, are negoti-ated; both parties must accept the terms. Because they involve negoti-ation and require students to assume responsibility for fulfilling their part of the bargain, contracts are probably best for older students.

Research suggests the following rules are useful for developing contingency contracts with students in the classroom:

- The initial contract payoff (reward) should be immediate.
- The initial contracts should call for and reward small approximations.
- Reward frequently with small amounts.
- The contract should call for and reward accomplishment rather than obedience.
- Reward the behavior after it occurs.
- The contract must be fair.
- The terms of the contract must be clear.
- The contract must be honest.
- The contract must be positive.
- Contracting as a method must be used systematically.

In sum, a good contract identifies the responsibilities of both par-ties and the consequences if the terms are not fulfilled.

Step VI

Apply Instructional Interventions for Specific Behaviors Exhibited in the Classroom by Students With Emotional and/or Behavioral Disorders

Instructional Interventions for Active Noncompliance

Examples of Behavior

- Actively refuses to follow directions (e.g., "no" or "I won't").
- Acts bored (e.g., "This is dumb" or rolls eyes).
- Does not finish assignments.
- Makes comments or walks away; leaves room.
- Spends lots of time looking for work or materials.
- Stalls or dawdles.
- Work is of poor quality (e.g., messy, carelessly done).

Desired Alternative Behavior(s)

- Asks for clarification if doesn't understand the task (e.g., by raising hand, waiting for teacher to finish speaking).
- Begins work within ___ minutes (or seconds) (e.g., gets materials out, opens books, begins task).
- Completes work neatly (e.g., handwriting is legible, paper is not wrinkled or smudged).
- Follows directions within ___ minutes (or seconds) without arguing or talking back.
- Shows good effort by having materials ready, beginning task within ___ minutes/seconds, attempting difficult tasks.
- Waits for turn to speak by raising hand, waiting for teacher acknowledgment.

General Instructional Strategies That Might Be Useful in Teaching the Desired Behavior(s)

- Ask yourself what the bottom line issue is. For instance, if it's getting the assignment done, then perhaps reinforce getting it done and work on neatness as the next step.
- Be gentle when cueing, correcting, redirecting, etc. The goal is to connect with the student, not push him further away.
- Break multistep activities into smaller steps with feedback and reinforcement along the way; break long-term assignments into smaller short-term tasks.
- Have clear expectations, allow student input, and review periodically.
- Offer choices in tasks and assignments. Focus on strengths and interests.
- Seat the student near the teacher, away from distractions, etc.
- Teach expectations and classroom procedures.
- Teach organizational skills and time management.
- Teach students problem-solving skills and decision-making skills.

Instructional Interventions for Attendance Problems

Examples of Behavior

- Gets far behind in schoolwork and gives up, cannot participate in on-going class activities, and/or cannot reasonably catch up.

Apply Instructional Interventions for Specific Behaviors Exhibited in the Classroom
by Students With Emotional and/or Behavioral Disorders

61

- Has poor/inconsistent attendance, even if excused.
- Is regularly late for class.
- Misses the whole class or day.
- Skips class but doesn't leave the school campus.

Desired Alternative Behavior(s)

- Attends school regularly (each class, entire day).
- Completes makeup work.
- Is on time for class and ready to work (has necessary materials).
- Is on time to class (define: In seat when bell rings? In room when bell rings?).

General Instructional Strategies That Might Be Useful in Teaching the Desired Behavior(s)

- Use a short-term intervention where the student's attendance is checked daily for some period of time (two or three weeks) and attendance is reinforced and rewarded. After that period of time, look at whether attendance has improved (so perhaps you can back off and only check weekly or every three–four days), stayed the same (maybe try it another week), or not improved and perhaps gotten worse (in which case you may be "back to the drawing board").
- Anticipate lateness. Seat the student near the door; have work on the desk and ready if/when the student arrives.
- Consider whether the school wants to have a consistent "on time" definition so that it is the same for all students.
- Contract for work based on amount of work to be completed rather than time limits.
- Depending on the underlying issues, refer the student to the guidance counselor, school social worker, or school psychologist. Consider whether there are community agencies that could be of help.
- Double up (spend more time on fewer subject areas so that the student can salvage something for the grading period).
- Have a plan for the student to make up the work; keep from overwhelming the student (independent study, demonstrating mastery rather than requiring every assignment, etc.).
- Have a task to be done as soon as students enter the room. It gives you time to set up, take attendance, do other housekeeping chores while keeping them busy. It can be a review of yesterday's lesson, a lead-in for today, journaling, creative writing, current events, etc.

- Involve the school nurse to make sure there are no serious health issues.
- Make sure the student knows what "on time" means; make sure student knows this for all classes.
- Provide a program that is motivating and reinforcing to the student, especially initially. Start with classes in which the student has skill or enjoys and build from there.
- Provide an alarm clock or give a wake-up call to the student.
- Reinforce progress, not just perfection.
- Reinforce the desired behavior.
- The issue may not be able to be addressed in the school alone. Are there other agencies, programs, or individuals who can be involved?
- Use service learning. Note that while the activity may be fun for the student (and not a "punishment" or negative consequence), the goal is to connect the student with the school and/or peers. Punishment makes the least sense in these instances.
- Use truancy abatement programs, such as providing a "neutral site" where students can catch up with work, deal with issues, and have some support for returning to school. Some communities have worked with the Boys/Girls Club to do this, and the program is often a cooperative effort among the school district, social services, and the club. Students may be brought to the site by the police or parents rather than being returned to the school building.
- Try to "prime" success for students when they return to school or attend by making sure the first tasks are motivating and successful so they feel competent and motivated to continue to attend.
- Use homework for bonus point for all kids.
- Work with student to find afterschool or partial-day employment if money is an issue; find ways for student to "earn" needed or desired items.

Instructional Interventions for Difficulty With Transitions

Examples of Behavior

- Actively resists activity change by having a tantrum, pushing, shoving, acting out, or verbal aggression.
- Has difficulty moving from one place or activity to another.
- Has difficulty starting and/or stopping an activity.

- Has difficulty with changes of routine (e.g., substitute teacher, fire drills, assemblies, shortened days due to weather or inservice times).
- Refuses to stop an activity, especially after being directed to do so.

Desired Alternative Behavior(s)

- Demonstrates organizational skills (e.g., prioritizes tasks, is able to leave tasks unfinished and return later to complete them).
- Follows teacher directions regarding schedule and change of activities.
- Keeps hands and feet to self (e.g., remains at least an arm's or leg's length away from others) when moving to another area or standing in line.
- Shifts from one activity to the next within ___ (amount of time).
- Uses appropriate conversation skills during unstructured times and transitions (e.g., acceptable tone and language with no swearing or shouting and at an acceptable volume for indoor settings).

General Instructional Strategies That Might Be Useful in Teaching the Desired Behavior(s)

- Actively engage students in learning activities to increase on-task behavior.
- Adjust demands depending on the time (e.g., student is on medications, and it is almost time for another dose; just before lunch; end of the day).
- Allow time for the student to process the request and respond.
- Foreshadow (e.g., "Three more minutes to finish up.").
- If transitioning from a favorite to a less favorite activity, prime the student for compliance by assigning a task with which the student will probably comply and then move to the next activity. For example, say, "Billy, bring me a dictionary, please," because the dictionary is close to Billy and he will probably bring it to you. Then say, "Thank you—now please sit at the large table." You can also reinforce Billy for complying with your first request, which might ease him into the next task.
- Implement a response cost/token economy.
- Post a daily schedule, making sure also to post changes.
- Use a peer mentoring/buddy system.
- Use cooperative learning.
- Use direct instruction.
- Use learning centers.

- Use modeling.
- Use role-playing.
- Use self-monitoring/checking.
- Use sensory integration techniques if the student may be over- or understimulated.
- Use social stories and comic book conversations.
- Vary instructional presentations.

Instructional Interventions for Disrespect to Teachers

Examples of Behavior

- Deliberately pushes the limits and openly defies the teacher.
- Draws inappropriate pictures, such as caricatures.
- Engages in name-calling or swearing.
- Engages in rudeness, talking back, or interrupting.
- Has "selective hearing" and ignores the teacher.
- Mimics, makes faces, or uses inappropriate gestures such as "the finger."
- Uses creative writing assignments to disrespect teachers.
- Walks away while the teacher is talking.
- Writes inappropriate messages on notebooks or folders.

Desired Alternative Behavior(s)

- Asks to take a break or self-timeout, using a prearranged phrase or nonverbal cue.
- Develops a script or cues to use and role play those alternatives.
- Disagrees respectfully (e.g., by using a preapproved script and by speaking in a conversational tone).
- Postpones discussion until time allows and student and teacher have had a chance to think.
- Talks or vents through journaling, writing, or drawing within previously determined guidelines (e.g., uses appropriate language, does not make threats).
- Uses active listening.

General Instructional Strategies That Might Be Useful in Teaching the Desired Behavior(s)

- Brainstorm and discuss real-life consequences of verbal and nonverbal disrespect.

- Give students time to think about how they want to fix the problem (e.g., making a verbal apology face-to-face, writing a letter, making a card, making restitution).
- Involve school counseling groups that focus on various topics (AODA, divorce, anger management, grief, stress relief, self esteem).
- Teach and model active listening.
- Teach anger management.
- Teach conflict resolution skills.
- Teach empathy/perspective taking.
- Teach stress relief strategies.
- Use *I* messages.
- Use peer mediation.
- Use scripting; role-play inappropriate behaviors and write better responses.
- Use video clips or vignettes as a basis for discussion (these help to relieve defensiveness).

Instructional Interventions for Classroom Disruption

Examples of Behavior

- Bothers another student, trying to engage the student in conversation.
- Gets out of seat and wanders around the room.
- Laughs/giggles at inappropriate times.
- Makes inappropriate noises (tapping pencil, humming, animal noises, play noises such as imitating airplanes or motorcycles, etc.).
- Throws things.
- Tries to engage other students in conversation.

Desired Alternative Behavior(s)

- Asks to move; asks for a break.
- Indicates they are unable to do the work.
- Raises hand or uses other teacher-approved cue (e.g., eye contact, writing on a slate, holding up a card) to answer during class time.
- Remains in seat for ____ minutes (or for duration of instructional activity) unless given teacher permission to get up.
- Remains on task (e.g., writing, reading, drawing) for a minimum of _____ minutes.
- Seeks help with a problem.

- Tells what *on-task* or *topic-related* means.
- Uses acceptable tone and volume of voice.
- Uses movement options/breaks without bothering other students or making noise.

General Instructional Strategies That Might Be Useful in Teaching the Desired Behavior(s)

- Adjust demands at critical times (e.g., just before lunch, end of the day, just before student needs medication, after an especially hard or stressful task).
- Develop classroom rules as a group.
- Give choices within classroom as opposed to teacher-directed only.
- Provide instruction on what to do when, turn taking, how to "signal," what cues to look for, and reading social situations and cues.
- Provide physical breaks, sensory breaks, and other movement options.
- Provide teacher- or student-assigned "jobs" in cooperative groups, giving everyone responsibility and encouraging following group expectations.
- Provide verbal cues for student to use to self-cue as a reminder of what he is supposed to be doing (e.g., "At this moment, am I . . . ?").
- Teach empathy/perspective taking.
- Teach errors in thinking.
- Teach social skills and provide opportunities to practice.
- Use erasable, individual slates or another type of board so student writes down question or answer she just has to express right now. The student can then show it to the teacher with little or no calling out or classroom disruption.

Instructional Interventions for Failure to Accept Responsibility for Own Behavior and/or Consequences for Misbehavior

Examples of Behavior

- Argues when confronted with a situation.
- Argues/resists consequences.
- Does not admit to wrongdoing.
- Does not take ownership for conflicts.

Desired Alternative Behavior(s)

- Accepts consequences without arguing or whining.
- Talks through the incident with a teacher or counselor and identifies alternatives for behavior (e.g., admitting responsibility, apologizing, making restitution).
- Tells how the behavior affects others.
- When presented with a problem situation, admits a mistake was made.
- When presented with wrongdoing, tells the truth regarding participation.

General Instructional Strategies That Might Be Useful in Teaching the Desired Behavior(s)

- Organize activities during recess.
- Teach a skill to the entire class, using peers for reinforcement and modeling, group contingencies, or reinforcement.
- Teach errors in thinking.
- Use behavioral contracting.
- Use overcorrection (requiring the student to repeatedly perform the appropriate behavior in the environment/situation where the misbehavior occurred and repeatedly reinforcing the student for the appropriate behavior).
- Use perspective taking/empathy training.
- Use restorative justice.
- Use role-playing.
- Use scripting.
- Use service learning.
- Use social stories.

Instructional Interventions for Interpersonal Relationships With Peers

Examples of Behavior

- Has difficulty interacting with peers (e.g., joining a group, playing a game, initiating and continuing social conversations, taking turns, etc.).
- Interrupts conversations.
- Is rude/impolite.
- Refuses to share and/or take turns.
- Tattles.

Desired Alternative Behavior(s)

- Independently shares toys/materials during group activities.
- Listens quietly while others talk and waits his or her turn to speak.
- Takes turns even while playing a game in informal settings.
- Uses pretaught steps in determining when to tell the teacher versus when to let it go untold (e.g., telling if there is a safety issue).
- Uses skill in various school settings (e.g., hall, lunchroom, study hall, all classrooms).

General Instructional Strategies That Might Be Useful in Teaching the Desired Behavior(s)

- Don't punish other students solely on the basis of tattling.
- Teach manners and politeness.
- Teach the difference between unnecessary tattling and reporting serious behavior.
- Use a gentle correction if behaviors are occasional or if reported behavior is not serious.
- Use behavior contracting.
- Use class meetings.
- Use precorrection/prompts.
- Use role-playing.
- Use supervised play and structured activities during recess or other free time.

Instructional Interventions for Out-of-Control Behaviors

Examples of Behavior

- Engages in self-injurious behavior or self-mutilation (e.g., scratching self, burning self with cigarette, etc.).
- Is a danger to self and/or others.
- Is unable to calm down, regroup, and continue after an outburst.
- Throws tantrums.

Desired Alternative Behavior(s)

- Identifies appropriate ways to behave in crisis/conflict.
- Problem-solves appropriate ways to regain control.

- Refrains from hurting self.
- Remains calm when faced with difficult situation.

General Instructional Strategies That Might Be Useful in Teaching the Desired Behavior(s)

- Ask, "What triggered the problem—how can I get the student back into being successful?"
- Discuss real-life consequences of verbal and nonverbal behaviors.
- Teach alternative activities to deal with built-up or escalating emotional tension.
- Teach anger management skills.
- Teach negotiation skills, conflict resolution strategies, and problem-solving skills.
- Teach relaxation or stress-reduction techniques.
- Use bibliotherapy.
- Use direct teaching of social skills.
- Use role-playing and modeling.
- Use social stories.

Instructional Interventions for Passive Resistance

Examples of Behavior

- "Just sits."
- Appears depressed (sad, flat affect, lethargic)
- Is disengaged.
- Is withdrawn.
- Refuses to work (passive, not disruptive).
- Sleeps in class.

Desired Alternative Behavior(s)

- Actively participates in classroom activities (e.g., stays awake, asks questions, talks when appropriate, participates in small-group activities).
- Completes assignments (with a minimum of __ percent accuracy, on time, turned in).

- Remains on-task (e.g., reading or writing, working on assignment) for ____ minutes.
- Resumes task within ____ seconds/minutes with no more than one prompt.

General Instructional Strategies That Might Be Useful in Teaching the Desired Behavior(s)

- Allow catching up. Have buddies give the students a "snapshot" of the day/activity/lesson they missed, call students at home to say you missed them, welcome them back.
- For students who are reluctant to ask questions or speak out, have them write questions on a piece of paper and then give them a written response. Be sure to compliment the student (e.g., "Good question," or, "Would you ask that question tomorrow in the large group?"). Also, you might send another student with the same question to the target student.
- Give choices (on homework, alternative testing options).
- Give extra credit (one point) for a pertinent question asked.
- Give students responsibility you know they will want and that will motivate them.
- Have students develop materials for other students (cross-age or same-age).
- Have the students help in a classroom where they have been successful in the past.
- Plug into the student's strengths, starting small and building on success.
- Provide passive breaks with time to relax, put head down, nap (if the student has a health or sleep-deprivation issue).
- Teach organization skills. This can be done in each class or in a homeroom or study hall by using different colored folders for each class and/or assignment notebooks.
- Teach social skills. Use small groups, cooperative learning, lab partners, cross-age tutoring, literature circles (each member has a role such as leader, recorder, vocabulary, etc., and members rotate roles).

Instructional Interventions for Not Respecting Property or Personal Space of Others

Examples of Behavior

- Damages another student's item.
- Fails to return an item loaned.

- Invades another's personal space.
- Takes things without permission that do not belong to the student.

Desired Alternative Behavior(s)

- Asks permission to use an item.
- Maintains a reasonable distance and respects the personal space of others.
- Returns borrowed item after use in reasonable/agreed-upon time.
- Returns borrowed item undamaged.

General Instructional Strategies That Might Be Useful in Teaching the Desired Behavior(s)

- Create and reinforce activities in which students work together for a common goal.
- Enforce restorative justice if items are damaged.
- Engage in activities to develop and improve self-esteem.
- Establish rules for sharing school materials and for bringing personal belongings to school/class (e.g., toys, portable electronics, etc.).
- Give tangible rewards and/or social praise for sharing.
- Keep a supply of school materials so that students have the materials they need.
- Teach social skills.
- Use a "glove tree" to make certain students have some winter clothing.
- Use behavior contracting.
- Use cooperative learning.
- Use smaller groups.

Instructional Interventions for Verbal Aggression

Examples of Behavior

- Engages in harassment and/or uses racial slurs.
- Engages in name-calling and/or put-downs.
- Engages in screaming or yelling or makes loud remarks.
- Makes sexual comments or gang comments.
- Makes threats and/or engages in bullying.
- Uses obscene or profane language.

Desired Alternative Behavior(s)

- Demonstrates respect to others by way of language used, tone of voice, and voice volume.
- Refrains from name-calling, threats, bullying, gang comments, sexual comments, and obscene language.
- Requests adult assistance to deal with conflict.
- Tells why certain language/comments are not acceptable and chooses acceptable alternatives.
- Uses acceptable language to give compliments and/or in social conversations. (You give examples of words or phrases student should use.)
- Uses conflict resolution/problem-solving strategies when in a conflict situation (identify problem, list options, identify consequences, choose one, evaluate effectiveness of choice, review/revise).
- Uses socially acceptable and respectful language.
- Walks away from conflicts and escalating situations.

General Instructional Strategies That Might Be Useful in Teaching the Desired Behavior(s)

- Build self-esteem so students won't feel a need to denigrate others.
- Communicate with parents about concerns and find out what they allow or don't allow with their child.
- Does the student know why comments are unacceptable? There may be cultural/ethnic issues. If so, talk to the student and explain the problem. Teach alternatives.
- Intervene early when student begins to make inappropriate comments to others so situation does not escalate.
- Model appropriate language at all times.
- Script and role-play better responses and appropriate language.
- Set expectations for an emotionally safe environment for all students.
- Teach anger management and stress relief.
- Use peer mediation.
- Use small-group counseling, teaching empathy, acceptance of differences, respect, etc.

Instructional Interventions for Verbal Outbursts

Examples of Behavior

- Argues with peers and/or adults.
- Calls out.

- Makes disruptive noises (humming, animal sounds, etc.).
- Screams or yells.

Desired Alternative Behavior(s)

- Accepts criticism without arguing.
- Asks for adult assistance to deal with teasing or other conflict.
- Develops a script or cues to use and role-plays or otherwise practices.
- Disagrees appropriately (e.g., using preselected statements).
- Discusses issue with adult or peer without becoming defensive.
- Follows classroom rules while participating in classroom activities.
- Ignores peers rather than teasing them.
- Lists ways in which his or her behavior affects others.
- Raises hand.
- Sits quietly during quiet times.
- Walks away from conflict.

General Instructional Strategies That Might Be Useful in Teaching the Desired Behavior(s)

- Allow movement breaks, sensory options, and other physical breaks.
- Give the student time to process and problem-solve.
- Teach and model desired behaviors.
- Teach anger management strategies.
- Teach conflict resolution strategies.
- Teach social skills.
- Teach stress relief.
- Use a token economy system.
- Use role-playing.
- Use social stories.

Step VII

Understand and Implement Classroom Management Strategies for Students With Specific Psychological Disorders

Child and Adolescent Mental Health and Schools

Mental health is how people think, feel, and act. It affects how they handle stress, relate to each other, and make decisions. It influences how they look at themselves, their lives, and others. Good mental health allows children to think clearly, develop socially, and learn new skills. Mental health in children and adolescents is the achievement of expected milestones (cognitive, social, and emotional) and effective coping skills and secure social relationships.

Doctors' offices and schools are important settings in which children's mental health issues can be recognized and addressed.

Schools may function as the de facto mental health system for many children and adolescents.

Students with a mental health diagnosis do not automatically qualify for special education under the Individuals with Disabilities Education Act (IDEA). Keep in mind that individualized education program (IEP) teams cannot make DSM-IV diagnoses and physicians cannot identify a child as having special education needs under IDEA. Schools may serve these students in their regular education programs by using a 504 Plan under the Americans with Disabilities Act.

Risk Factors

Usually a combination of risk factors is at work. They can be biological and/or psychosocial.

Biological

- Genes that carry a predisposition or risk for an illness
- Environmental (prenatal damage, poverty, deprivation, abuse and neglect, trauma, and poor nutrition)
- Problems caused by injury, illness, exposure to toxins

Adverse Psychosocial Development

- Stressful life events leading to a negative change in the child's circumstances (dysfunctional family life, severe discord, parent psychopathology or criminality, inconsistent discipline, lack of loving relationship with at least one parent, maladaptive influence of peers and siblings)
- Economic hardship
- Exposure to violence
- Poor caregiving

How common are mental health problems in children? Consider the following data from the Surgeon General's Report and the President's New Freedom Commission:

- Among children ages 9–17, almost 21 percent have a diagnosable mental or addictive disorder; of those, 11 percent have a significant impairment, and 5 percent have an extreme functional impairment.
- Only one in five children or adolescents gets mental health services in any given year.

- Children of depressed parents are more than three times as likely to experience depression.
- Parental depression increases a child's risk of anxiety disorders, conduct disorders, and alcoholism.
- Of 21-year-olds with mental health disorders, 74 percent had prior problems.

Mental Disorders With Onset in Children and Adolescents

- Anxiety disorders (e.g., obsessive-compulsive disorder (OCD), generalized anxiety disorder, phobias, panic disorder)
- Attention deficit and disruptive behavior disorders
- Autism and other pervasive developmental disorders
- Eating disorders
- Elimination disorders
- Learning and communication disorders
- Mood disorders (e.g., depression, bipolar disorder)
- Schizophrenia

Warning Signs That a Child or Adolescent May Need Mental Health Services

Emotions

- Crying or overreaction
- Excessive concern with physical problems or appearance
- Excessive worry or anxiety
- Extreme anger most of the time
- Extreme fearfulness
- Fear of being out of control
- Feeling life is "too much"; thoughts of suicide
- Sadness or hopelessness for no reason that does not go away
- Unable to get over a loss or death
- Worthlessness or guilt

Big Changes

- Avoiding other people and isolating oneself
- Daydreaming too much and not finishing tasks
- Decline in school performance
- Hearing voices that cannot be explained
- Loss of interest in things once enjoyed
- Poor grades despite strong efforts

- Repeated refusal to go to school or take part in normal childhood/
  adolescent activities
- Unexplained changes in eating or sleeping habits

Experiences/Behaviors

- Behaving without regard for other people
- Bingeing and purging; abusing laxatives
- Breaking the law; abusing the rights of others
- Difficulty concentrating and/or making decisions
- Excessive dieting or exercising
- Excessive worry about doing something "bad"
- Hyperactivity or excessive fidgeting
- Life-threatening or other dangerous behavior
- Need to wash or perform certain routines hundreds of times
  each day
- Persistent disobedience or aggression
- Persistent nightmares
- Racing thoughts
- Setting fires
- Torturing or killing animals
- Using alcohol or other drugs

Role of the School

- What are the functions of "mental health services in the
  school"?
- Promoting positive mental health and social and emotional
  development
- Addressing mental health problems as they present barriers to
  learning
- Providing linkages to community agencies and resources
- Delivering mental health resources within or in association
  with school settings
- Providing school resources for meeting student mental health
  needs
- Delivering primary prevention services
  o Alcohol and other drug abuse (AODA) education
  o Conflict resolution
  o Health classes
  o Parent involvement
  o Support for transitions

- Delivering early intervention
  - ○ Accommodations for learning and behavior concerns
  - ○ AODA counseling
  - ○ Dropout prevention
  - ○ Pregnancy prevention/school-age parent programs
  - ○ Violence prevention
  - ○ Work programs

- Providing care for severe and chronic problems
  - ○ Special education
  - ○ Communication with families
  - ○ Coordination with community service providers
  - ○ Crisis intervention

    Restoring calm, problem-solving, collecting information

    Moving the student away from being a victim

    Connecting the student with immediate support

    Taking care of the caretakers

    Providing for the aftermath

How can we differentiate between manifestations of the illness and learned behaviors?

- Learn about the symptoms of the illness in general. Talk to parents and the therapist about how the illness is manifested in this particular child/adolescent. What are reasonable needs or behaviors? How recent is the diagnosis? If the diagnosis was some time ago, what changes in behavior have taken place? What is normal for the child's chronological age and developmental level? How should you expect the illness to impact on those typical milestones?
- Conduct a functional behavioral analysis (FBA) to help determine triggers/antecedents, as well as maintaining consequences. This includes developing a hypothesis as to whether the behavior is symptomatic, learned, or a combination. Observe the student; gather anecdotal information; and interview teachers, other staff, parents, the student (if appropriate), and the therapist. Then develop a behavior plan that can be tested to see if the behavior can be modified.
- Consider whether the behavior is based on the illness but goes beyond what might be expected. For example, a student with poor impulse control and hyperactivity may need to move around and should be allowed to do so, but the movement can

be structured within a particular area, time frame, and so on. The student is not allowed to run around freely, disrupting the learning environment—that is the behavioral, or learned part, which can be addressed.

- Keep in mind that you may not be able to differentiate between manifestations of the illness and learned behaviors. In that case, consider the behavior a manifestation of the illness and proceed accordingly.

If students refuse to take their prescribed medications, we can work with parents and therapists to do the following:

- Reinforce the medication's benefits.
- Set up a reward system for compliance.
- Talk honestly about the side effects with older students and support them in dealing with those (weight loss efforts, good nutrition, etc.).
- Conduct an FBA to determine why the student is refusing. Is the student seeking attention? Is the refusal a way to gain a feeling of control in life? Is it to avoid side effects? Is it because the medications are a reminder of a deficit or that the student feels "abnormal"? Is it due to denial of the illness?
- Honor the child's privacy by not announcing that the student should come to the office to take medications.

Summary

Following are the costs of not intervening early and promptly:

- *Lost productivity.* Parents have to miss work if called to school about problems or if they must stay at home to care for the child. Children who drop out or are suspended or expelled often experience unemployment.
- *Lost learning.* Children miss school and fall behind academically.
- *Diminished quality of life.* Problems tend to last for a long time, creating long-term problems for the individual and that person's family.
- *Safety.* Students with mental health issues are often at great risk for substance abuse and involvement in the juvenile justice system.

Schools are on the front lines for identifying students with possible mental health needs and for providing prevention and intervention within the school setting.

Classroom Management for Students With Anxiety Disorders

Overview

- Anxiety disorders include generalized anxiety disorder, phobias, panic disorder, obsessive-compulsive disorder (OCD), and posttraumatic stress disorder (PTSD). *Anxiety* is a feeling that one's safety or well-being is in danger.

- Risk factors for anxiety disorders include shyness in unfamiliar situations and having parent(s) with anxiety disorders (although it is unclear whether the parents contribute biology, environment, or both). Children who have experienced high stress are at high risk for anxiety disorders; stressors may include moving, changing schools, failure, loss of close relative, divorce, and bodily injury. Also, between the ages of six and eight children normally become less afraid of the dark and monsters and more concerned about school performance and social relationships; if that isn't happening, there may be cause for concern.

- One in ten children/adolescents may have an anxiety disorder. Among adolescents, more girls than boys are affected. Likewise, for phobias, girls have a higher incidence rate than boys at all ages.

- Anxiety is normal at some developmental stages (for example, children from eight months to preschool age often display separation anxiety).

- Social phobias include fear of public speaking, fear of social interactions, fear of using public bathrooms (sometimes called "bashful bladder"), or fear of eating or drinking in public. Social phobias generally have an onset in childhood or adolescence and may include physical complaints, such as headache or stomach pains. Social phobias are often not noticed in school because the students may be quiet and not overt behavior problems. Social phobias tend to be chronic and is often comorbid with depression, substance abuse, and other anxiety disorders.

- Panic disorder is often comorbid with agoraphobia (fear of losing control in a public place), depression, and other anxiety disorders. Panic disorders are more likely to start in late adolescence or adulthood. The courses of panic disorder and agoraphobia are chronic.

- Treatment for anxiety disorders is usually a combination of individual psychotherapy, family therapy, medications, behavioral treatments, and/or consultation with the school.

- If untreated, an anxiety disorder can lead to missed school, poor peer relationships, and abuse of alcohol and other drugs.
- About one-half of children and adolescents with an anxiety disorder have a second anxiety disorder or another mental health issue, such as depression.

Symptoms

- No typical developmental stage or phase
- Being clingy
- Being frequently absent from school
- Being overly quiet, compliant, and eager to please.
- Experiencing many worries about things before they happen or constant worrying.
- Fearing embarrassment or making errors
- Fearing new situations
- Feeling apprehension with no discernible cause
- Feeling overly tense and uptight
- Feeling that something bad will happen and a lack of control over it
- Having frequent bouts of tears
- Having low self-esteem
- Having many physical complaints
- Having nightmares and/or trouble sleeping
- Having panic attacks
- Seeking a lot of reassurance

Generalized Anxiety Disorder

- Being very self-conscious
- Experiencing extreme, unrealistic worry
- Experiencing stomachaches or other physical symptoms with no apparent physical basis
- Feeling tense
- Having a high need for reassurance

Phobias

- Feeling an unrealistic, excessive fear of a situation or an object
- In the case of social phobias, feeling afraid of being harshly judged; extreme shyness; fear of public performance, group gatherings, public restrooms, etc.
- In the case of specific phobias, feeling afraid of animals, storms, being confined in small spaces, etc.

Panic Disorders

- Experiencing panic attacks, time-limited, intense episodes of dread accompanied by physical symptoms such as intense fear, pounding heart, sweating, dizziness, nausea, and/or fear of imminent death
- Fearing another attack

The table below lists typical fears or causes of anxiety for children at various age levels. Ask: Is my student's anxiety typical for a child of that age? Is the anxiety seen across many situations, or is it limited to a specific situation, such as speaking in front of the class? Is the anxiety of a long-term nature, or has it occurred recently? Are events in the child's life causing stress and pressure? Is the anxiety a sign of a larger problem, such as home and family difficulties? Is the anxiety having a great effect on the child's personal, social, and school functioning?

Age	Anxiety
6–7	Strange or loud noises, separation from parents, being lost, being alone at night, ghosts or other supernatural beings, being hurt by or rejected by specific individuals at school
7–8	The dark and dark places, not being liked, real-life catastrophes such as seen on TV, being late for school, being left out of family or school events, being hurt or rejected by specific individuals at school
8–9	Failure in school, sports, or in activities of play; personal humiliation; being caught in a lie; being the victim of violence; parents fighting or being hurt
9–11	Failure in school or at sports, becoming sick, animals larger than humans or that may attack humans, heights, sinister people such as murderers
11–13	Failure in school or sports or social situations, looking strange, being robbed, sex (being attacked, either being repellant to others or attractive to others), death or life-threatening illness, being fooled or brainwashed

Possible School Interventions

Possible School Interventions for Students With Anxiety Disorders

- Be consistent, providing a consistent routine and schedule, discipline, and feedback.
- Provide a supportive environment: acknowledge that you know things are difficult for the student and that you understand.
- Validate the student's feelings: the feelings are real to the student.
- Focus on positives; build on success.
- Help the student to feel in control by allowing choices and providing a place the student can go and someone to talk with if overwhelmed.
- Conduct a functional behavioral assessment (FBA) to determine triggers and critical times, activities, etc.
- Avoid excessive, harsh, or unusual discipline.
- Set realistic, attainable goals.
- Model calmness, good decision-making processes, and confidence.
- Teach relaxation skills and decision-making skills.
- Help the student improve self-worth, self-concept, and self-esteem.
- If possible, before the start of the school year, allow the student to meet you and other new staff. Set up a buddy system if it will help the student to feel more comfortable.
- Work for smooth transitions by foreshadowing what is to come, changes in routine, and so on.
- Minimize the pressure or stress on the student by matching work to ability, providing extra help, monitoring closely to be sure the student isn't overwhelmed, using activities that are motivating and interesting to that student, and building on strengths and interests.
- Be flexible with time lines and workload.
- Teach to the students' strengths so that they will feel more confident.
- Encourage good attendance but be flexible with scheduling (e.g., shorten days if a student is experiencing a difficult period) and have a plan for students to make up work so that they don't feel overwhelmed upon returning.
- Understand that problems may get worse before they get better; support and encourage the student.
- Use cognitive-behavioral interventions.
- Teach stress management. One model is COPE:
  - o **C**alming nerves (learning to relax, return to calm or self-control)
  - o **O**riginating an imaginative plan (gaining insight and understanding into the anxiety and creating an antianxiety plan)
  - o **P**ersisting in the face of obstacles and failure
  - o **E**valuating and adjusting the plan

Summary

- If untreated, anxiety disorders can conflict with job requirements, family relationships, and/or other daily activities.
- Barriers to treatment include awareness, accessibility, and affordability.
- Successful coping has three components:

    Self-worth. The individual is more likely to have the confidence needed to attempt new things.

    Security. The individual has others to rely on.

    Control. The individual knows she can cope.

Students with an anxiety disorder diagnosis do not automatically qualify for special education under the Individuals with Disabilities Education Act (IDEA). Keep in mind that IEP teams cannot make DSM-IV diagnoses and physicians cannot identify a child as having special education needs under IDEA. If a student with a mental health diagnosis does not qualify for special education under IDEA, schools may serve these students in their regular education programs or by using a 504 Plan.

Communication with the family and the student's mental health team (physician, therapist, etc.) is critical. It is important for school personnel to know the possible side effects of medications the student is taking, as well as how the disease is manifested for that student.

Flexibility is key to working with students who have a mental illness. Schedules, workloads, expectations, and time lines may need to be adjusted as the student experiences more or fewer symptoms.

Classroom Management for Students With Bipolar Disorder

Overview

- Bipolar disorder (sometimes called manic-depression) is marked by extreme changes in mood, energy, thinking, and behavior. *Hypomania* is a milder form of mania that still causes difficulties for the individual but generally does not require hospitalization.
- Many children diagnosed with attention deficit disorder (ADHD) have early-onset bipolar disorder instead of, or along with, ADHD. Likewise, up to one-third of children and adolescents diagnosed with depression may actually have early-onset bipolar disorder.

- There are overlapping symptoms and diagnostic confusion among bipolar disorder and (among others) ADHD, Tourette's, obsessive-compulsive disorder (OCD), oppositional defiant disorder (ODD), conduct disorder, eating disorders, schizophrenia, and autism spectrum disorders/pervasive development disorders (ASD/PDD).
- Of children with early-onset bipolar disorder, 80 percent have bilineal transmission (substance abuse and mood disorders on both sides of their family). A student is at higher risk if one or both parents and/or siblings have the illness. When one parent has bipolar disorder, the risk is 15–30 percent that the child will have it; when both parents have it, the risk is 50–75 percent. The disease can skip generations, and symptoms may be different for each individual. The risk for identical twins is 70 percent, for siblings and fraternal twins, the risk is 15–25 percent greater than for unrelated children.
- In every generation since World War II, there has been a higher incidence and an earlier age of onset of bipolar disorder. Bipolar children have, on average, their first episode 10 years earlier than their parents' generation did. No one knows why this is so.
- Children later diagnosed with bipolar disorder were often difficult to settle and slept erratically as early as infancy. They were reported to be "clingy" and often had uncontrollable tantrums or rages.
- Puberty may be a trigger. Likewise, loss or another traumatic event may trigger mania or depression.
- It is not known how common this illness is in children, but 1–2 percent of adults are affected. About half of adults with bipolar disorder had their first episode before age 17. About 20 percent had their first episode between the ages of 10 and 14, and about 10 percent between the ages of 5 and 9.
- In adults, bipolar disorder is more common in females; among children and adolescents, it is more common in males.
- Bipolar disorder in children and adolescents is more severe and more difficult to treat than it is in adults.
- In adolescents, the symptoms may more closely resemble those of adults than those of children.
- Treatment often includes mood-stabilizing medications, even though little research has been done on their use in children and adolescents. Examples include lithium, Depakote (divalproex), and Tegretol (carbamazepine). Initial side effects, which may subside, include headaches, excessive thirst, frequent

urination, and gastrointestinal upset. Other side effects may include weight gain, acne, and short-term memory problems. In addition to medications, treatment should include psychotherapy and counseling to help patients accept their illness and learn ways to help themselves.

- A student with bipolar disorder may be dealing with three separate issues: the depression, the mania, and the cycling.
- A majority of teens with untreated bipolar disorder abuse alcohol and other drugs.
- School avoidance may be an issue as students find themselves falling further and further behind and become more and more frustrated. In addition, peers may reject the student due to bizarre or cyclical behavior, and this may also result in school avoidance.

Symptoms

- Children with early-onset bipolar cycle back-and-forth with few "well" times between (unlike adults). They may have rapid cycling (e.g., four times per year), ultrarapid cycling (weekly or monthly), or ultradian cycling (daily). Children with ultradian cycling may experience "mixed states" due to the rapidity of mood changes.
- Symptoms may include the following:
  o Dare-devil behavior

  o Daydreaming

  o Deficits in executive functioning skills (e.g., problem solving, working memory, attention, self-control, motor sequencing)

  o Depression

  o Difficulty transitioning from one activity to another due to inflexibility

  o Difficulty with breaking complex tasks into manageable pieces

  o Disorganization

  o Extreme or explosive rages or tantrums

  o Fluctuating energy levels; difficulty getting up and getting going in the morning

  o Grandiose behavior (e.g., thinking that rules do not apply)

  o Impulsivity, hyperactivity, distractibility, agitation

  o Inappropriate or precocious sexual behavior (hypersexual behavior—the sex drive is imperative), especially when hypomanic (mild degree of mania)

- o Irritability

- o Lying

- o Night terrors (dreams of blood and violence), which may explain why the child says shocking or cruel things (imagery of the nightmares is spilling over to the conscious mind)

- o Oppositional behavior

- o Peer relationship problems, missing social cues and boundaries

- o Racing thoughts

- o Rapid mood swings

- o Sensitivity to stimuli such as noises, smells, etc. or to hot and cold

- o Separation anxiety

- o Short-term memory problems

- o Suicidal thoughts and actions

- o Very strong and frequent cravings for sweets or other carbohydrates

Why is there difficulty in diagnosing early-onset bipolar disorder?

No lab tests are available.

Symptoms overlap with those of other conditions.

Developmental factors may be confusing; what *is* "normal" at a particular age or developmental level?

Adult criteria are applied, but the rapid cycling in children may mean that the duration of symptoms is not present.

The initial episode may be depressive and treated that way; antidepressant medications may induce hypomania (mild degree of mania), as might stimulant medications used for ADHD.

Issues for adolescents include the following:

- Some mood-stabilizing medications can cause acne or weight gain, contributing to already low self-esteem.
- At times, teens may be hypersexual.
- Adolescents with bipolar disorder are more prone to addiction.
- They may engage in risky behaviors, such as driving fast or using alcohol or other drugs.

Possible School Interventions

Possible School Interventions for Students With Bipolar Disorder

- Schedule key academics later in the day if the student has difficulty getting going in the morning.
- Arrange for a delayed start or shortened day if the student has difficulty waking up or getting to school in the morning.
- Provide a flexible program to allow for changes in school performance due to the cyclical nature of the illness.
- Use a daily assignment notebook.
- Remind the student at the end of the day to take work home if necessary.
- Provide a second set of books and materials at home if student is absent or if student often forgets to take them home.
- Modify or eliminate homework assignments according to the student's changing energy level and ability to concentrate.
- Reduce/modify academic demands as appropriate.
- Use books on tape.
- Break assignments into manageable chunks.
- Allow extended time on tests to reduce anxiety.
- Allow for alternate testing such as oral tests.
- Provide assistive technology, such as a calculator for math or a word processor for written work.
- Be sure that those working with the student understand the side effects of medication, as well as the symptoms that may impact school performance. For example, some medications used for bipolar disorder may cause difficulty with concentration.
- Identify a place where the student can go to regain self-control if needed and allow the student to use it.
- Arrange a private signal for the student to use when needing to leave the room.
- Set weekly goals so the student can see short-term success.
- Conduct a functional behavioral assessment (FBA) to determine triggers or antecedents to loss of control and adjust accordingly; also to help determine what is learned behavior and what is a symptom of the illness.
- Teach social skills.
- Teach coping skills.
- Work with the student to avert social problems.
- Stay alert as to whether the student is being bullied and follow up as needed.
- Keep in frequent touch with parents and therapists.
- Foreshadow transitions.
- Provide adaptive physical education to avoid overstimulation; excuse the student on hot days if student is easily overheated; use individual workouts or other healthful activities; provide one-on-one coaching; allow access to fluids if overheating/ dehydration is an issue.

Possible School Interventions for Students With Bipolar Disorder

- Check regularly on students' progress so that they don't get impossibly behind.
- Excuse the student from public speaking and presentations if anxiety is an issue; allow for one-to-one presentation, videotape, etc.
- Cut down on distractions.
- Schedule the student with instructors who are willing to be flexible and can adjust to the cyclical nature of the illness.
- Use curricula that encourage creativity.
- Provide tutoring if there are extended absences.
- If the student is returning from hospitalization or time out of school due to the illness, plan for a successful return to school by reducing stress and providing accommodations as necessary.
- Allow the student to take a break if upset or if inappropriate behaviors are beginning to escalate.
- Work with the parents and the therapist to understand how the disorder is manifested for this student.
- If thirst due to medication is an issue, allow the student to have a water bottle or access to a drinking fountain.
- If the student needs to urinate frequently due to medication, allow bathroom access.
- Set clear boundaries and expectations; avoid "surprises" for the student.
- Keep in mind that stress can trigger symptoms and plan accordingly.
- Plan for options if the student refuses to take prescribed medication or if there is a crisis; you may need different options for manic periods, depressive periods, and times when the student is doing well.

Summary

- Positive outcomes to hope for include the student's finding effective medication(s), particularly medication that is both effective and has minimal side effects and continues to work over time, and that the student keeps taking the prescribed medication(s) and adheres to the treatment plan.
- Reasons for optimism include the following:
  - There are medications that help.
  - Research on early-onset bipolar disorder is being conducted with the hope of finding more answers.
  - Internet resources are available that can help families, school, and children.
  - Advocates and agencies are becoming more aware of this population's needs (e.g., legislative action, insurance coverage, and so on).
  - Bipolar disorder is treatable.

Students with a bipolar disorder diagnosis do not automatically qualify for special education under the Individuals with Disabilities Education Act (IDEA). Keep in mind that IEP teams cannot make DSM-IV diagnoses and physicians cannot identify a child as having special education needs under IDEA. If a student with a mental health diagnosis does not qualify for special education under IDEA, schools may serve these students in their regular education programs or by using a 504 Plan.

Communication with the family and the student's mental health team (physician, therapist, etc.) is critical. It is important for school personnel to know the possible side effects of medications the student is taking, as well as how the disease is manifested for that student.

Flexibility is key to working with students who have a mental illness. Schedules, workloads, expectations, and time lines may need to be adjusted as the student experiences more or fewer symptoms.

Classroom Management for Students With Borderline Personality Disorder (BPD)

Overview

- A relatively new diagnosis, BPD has only been recognized since 1980. Some claim there is no such thing as BPD, but many research studies and clinical papers show it is a valid mental illness.

- Symptoms may be similar to those of anxiety disorders, schizophrenia, and other personality disorders; therefore, borderline personality disorder is often difficult to diagnose.
- BPD can be comorbid with posttraumatic stress disorder (PTSD), depression, bipolar disorder, passive-aggressive personality disorder, anxiety disorders, obsessive-compulsive disorder (OCD), attention deficit disorder (ADHD), and others.
- Causes are generally both environmental and genetic, including chemical imbalances and childhood trauma (abuse, neglect); about three-quarters of persons with BPD have a history of sexual abuse.
- BPD occurs in about 2 percent of the general population. BPD is often diagnosed in adolescents and young adults. About 75 percent of those diagnosed with BPD are female.
- BPD is treated with a combination of therapy and medications to reduce related anxiety, depression, etc.
- Individuals with BPD generally feel shame, guilt, emptiness, and/or emotional distress; those with antisocial personality disorder (APD) usually do not. An individual with APD is sometimes called a sociopath. To be identified with APD, the individual must have evidenced a conduct disorder before age 15 and be at least 18 years of age, among other symptoms. Therefore, APD is rarely seen in the PreK–12 school system.
- Those with BPD have one of the highest risks of suicide of all mental health conditions.
- The behaviors of someone with BPD may be internalizing (trying to hurt oneself), externalizing (trying to shift the pain to others), or both.
- Individuals with BPD are often intelligent and witty and may appear to be competent and friendly to those who are not closely acquainted with them.
- When someone with BPD expresses a "want," it generally is what that person wants at the moment.
- Patients whose outcomes were better than average tended to have high intelligence, unusual artistic talent, physical attractiveness (women), and obsessive-compulsive traits that reinforced self-discipline and the ability to self-structure time (both work and leisure).

Symptoms

- For students under 18, symptomatic behaviors displayed for at least one year and not be more appropriately explained by developmental level, substance abuse, depression, and/or an eating disorder

- Unstable interpersonal relationships that fluctuate between positive and negative (known as "splitting"—a person who is considered "all good" one day can be considered "all bad" the next day, or even later the same day); stormy and intense relationships; "forgetting" about the negative when the individual becomes positive
- Being easily provoked; explosive
- Being extremely suspicious of others
- Creating crises to avoid being alone; making frantic efforts to avoid being abandoned (real or imagined abandonment); having a fear of abandonment
- Cutting, burning, scratching self
- Demanding constant attention and/or making unreasonable demands
- Denying responsibility for actions; blaming others for problems
- Engaging in impulsive/bingeing behavior (e.g., spending, eating, sex, reckless driving, shoplifting, abuse of alcohol/other drugs)
- Engaging in provocative behavior
- Experiencing extreme mood swings
- Experiencing occasional dissociation (daydreaming, temporary removal from reality)
- Expressing extreme boredom
- Extreme insecurity and feelings of being flawed or damaged
- Having a poor sense of identity/self
- Having difficulty with personal limits, both one's own and those of others
- Having extreme views with a black-and-white view of things (no shades of gray)
- Making frequent threats/attempts of suicide
- Putting down, criticizing, and belittling others
- Taking what others say or do and twisting it to use against those others
- Trying to control others because of feeling out of control oneself
- Possibly being
  o narcissistic (being intolerant of criticism, feeling little or no empathy, having self-important feelings;
  o antisocial (reckless, callous, deceitful); and/or
  o histrionic (self-indulgent, self-dramatizing)

Possible School Interventions

Possible School Interventions for Students With Borderline Personality Disorder

- Avoid responding with anger—stay calm and composed.
- Try to avoid personalizing the behaviors—they are part of the illness.
- Talk later—you can't reason with someone in a rage.
- Agree to disagree where possible.
- Don't beg and threaten—make positive, declarative statements.
- Have firm schedules and consistent routines.
- Have clear expectations for the student and be sure the student understands what to expect of others.
- Consistently enforce limits.
- Consider providing outlets for negative feelings, such as music, art, dance/movement, yoga, journaling, or other creative writing.
- Encourage good nutrition and exercise.
- Teach stress reduction and relaxation techniques.
- Avoid power struggles with the student.
- Give choices when you can to give the student "control."
- Be aware of your own "hot buttons" and try to stay in control when the student tries to push them.
- Use cognitive-behavioral interventions (e.g., errors in thinking, good thinking, correct thinking) to reinforce positive traits, experiences, support from others, etc.
- Keep notes on patterns of behavior so you can predict problems and respond accordingly.
- Conduct an FBA to help predict problem situations, as well as the function of inappropriate behaviors. Those with BPD often try to control others or situations because they feel out of control themselves, for example.
- Defuse situations by using *I* messages (e.g., "when you do ____, I feel ____."); remain neutral and listen and restate what the person said.
- Reinforce that having emotions or feeling a certain way is okay—the problem is what how individual is acting on those feelings or emotions.
- During confrontations, it is important to state the facts and remain neutral and calm. Try the SET model:
  - *Support.* Pledge to try to be of help with an emphasis on the speaker's feelings ("I am worried about you.").
  - *Empathy.* Acknowledge the other's feelings without being sympathetic ("How awful you must feel."
  - *Truth.* Emphasize that the individual is responsible for herself ("What are you going to do?" "These are the consequences of what happened—what are you going to do?").

(Continued)

(Continued)

Possible School Interventions for Students With Borderline Personality Disorder

• If the student's rage is out of control, have a crisis plan.	• If the student criticizes, verbally attacks, or tries to manipulate: ○ *Don't defend.* You won't win the argument. ○ *Don't deny.* This can quickly turn into "did not/did too." ○ *Don't counterattack.* The best way to defuse the attack is not to allow oneself to be pulled in. ○ *Don't withdraw.* If you feel attacked, you can leave the immediate situation. However, in the long run, don't remain silent and passive and allow the individual to succeed.

Summary

Although BPD is a challenging illness, there are reasons for optimism:

- Individuals with BPD can recover, but it is a slow process. The individual must want to recover, and recovery may involve a very painful process of facing a history of abuse or shame.
- Early intervention yields better outcomes. For example, if the individual has not yet permanently damaged interpersonal connections, he or she may still be able to "mend fences."

Students with a borderline personality diagnosis do not automatically qualify for special education under the Individuals with Disabilities Education Act (IDEA). Keep in mind that IEP teams cannot make DSM-IV diagnoses and physicians cannot identify a child as having special education needs under IDEA. If a student with a mental health diagnosis does not qualify for special education under IDEA, schools may serve these students in the regular education programs or by using a 504 Plan.

Communication with the family and the student's mental health team (physician, therapist, etc.) is critical. It is important for school personnel to know the possible side effects of medications the student is taking, as well as how the disease is manifested for that student.

Flexibility is key to working with students who have a mental illness. Schedules, workloads, expectations, and time lines may need to be adjusted as the student experiences more or fewer symptoms.

Classroom Management for Students With Depression

Overview

- Depression is not a character flaw, normal "blue" feelings, or a passing phase.
- *Depression* may also be called "major depression" or "clinical depression."
- Two-thirds of students with depression have comorbid diagnoses, including anxiety, conduct disorder, ODD (oppositional defiant disorder), AODA (alcohol and other drug abuse), phobias, OCD (obsessive-compulsive disorder), ADHD (attention deficit hyperactivity disorder), learning disorders, and delinquent behavior.
- *Dysthymia* is a less severe form of depression in which symptoms are less evident and may appear chronic, lasting for more than two years.
- Risk factors include a family history of mental illness or suicide; abuse (physical, emotional, sexual); loss of a parent at an early age (due to death, divorce, or abandonment).
- Until the 1980s, children were rarely considered to suffer from depression. However, according to the National Institute for Mental Health (2001), up to 2.5 percent of children and up to 8.3 percent of adolescents suffer from depression. As many as 5 percent of children and adolescents could be diagnosed at any one time.
- One-quarter to one-half of children and adolescents in psychiatric treatment centers are seen for depression and related issues. The three most common mood disorders in children and adolescents are major depression, dysthymia, and bipolar disorder.
- For children, there is an equal risk of depression in boys and in girls; in adolescence, twice as many girls as boys are diagnosed.
- Fewer than half of those with depression get appropriate treatment. Cognitive behavioral therapy and interpersonal therapy have been shown to be effective in treating depression in children and adolescents. Psychotherapy is the first choice of treatments and may be combined with medications.

- There is very little research on the use of antidepressant medication with children. Bipolar disorder should be ruled out before antidepressants for depression or stimulants are prescribed, as those medications can trigger mania.
- Suicide is a frequent and direct result of depression: up to 7 percent of adolescents with major depression may eventually commit suicide.
- Children and adolescents recover from a bout of depression at very high rates, but recurrence is likely, with 70 percent having another episode within five years.
- Children may have difficulty describing abstract emotions and feelings, making diagnosis of depression challenging.
- School refusal/school phobia (children who do not attend because of emotional distress) is often comorbid with depression.
- Students who are depressed may have difficulty with information processing, cognitive distortions, low self-esteem, and a perception of themselves as helpless.

Symptoms

- Being overly sensitive
- Being rejected by peers
- Being unable to concentrate
- Eating too much or too little
- Engaging in outbursts of yelling, crying, or extreme irritability
- Engaging in reckless behavior, including alcohol or other drug abuse
- Exhibiting deteriorating school performance
- Exhibiting increased anger or hostile behavior
- Exhibiting internalizing behaviors, such as timidity, anxiety, lack of interest in activities or people, victim mentality, rejection by peers, isolating self, verbalizing sadness. Note that internalizing behaviors are often overlooked because the student is not acting out or disruptive.
- Exhibiting social isolation from family and friends
- Feeling decreased interest in things that were once favorites
- Feeling extreme boredom
- Feeling guilt about past events
- Feeling hopelessness, worthlessness; making negative statements about self
- Frequently feeling sad, crying
- Having difficulty concentrating
- Having low energy

- Having negative self-esteem and/or excessive guilt feelings
- Having thoughts or threats of suicide; engaging in self-harming behavior
- Making frequent vague complaints of physical ailments, such as headaches or stomachaches
- Neglecting appearance and hygiene
- Running away
- Sleeping too much or too little; sleeping in class
- In preschool children, the following may be indicative of a mood disorder:
  o Becoming spontaneously tearful or irritable (e.g., not because they didn't get their way)
  o Being self-destructive
  o Lacking "bounce"
  o Looking somber, almost ill

- In elementary-aged children and adolescents, the following may be indicative of a mood disorder:
  o Academic difficulties, worsening school performance
  o Disruptive behavior
  o Increased irritability and aggression
  o Nothing seeming to please them
  o Peer problems
  o Saying they hate themselves and everything around them
  o Suicidal threats

- Keep in mind anger, irritability, aggressiveness, tantrums, and restlessness may all be symptoms of depression.

Possible School Interventions

Possible School Interventions for Students With Depression

• Create a positive, supportive environment. • Improve the student's self-worth, sense of self-control, optimism. • Avoid aversives (punishment, getting "tough"). • Develop initial success and build on it; help student to avoid hopelessness.	• Be aware of, and pay attention to, the warning signs of suicide (e.g., threats of suicide, obsession with death, writings or drawings related to death, dramatic personality changes, changes in eating or sleeping, deteriorating appearance, declining school performance, giving away belongings, other strange or unusual behavior).

(Continued)

(Continued)

Possible School Interventions for Students With Depression

- Give school credit based on work completed, not on the calendar.
- Ease the student's return after weekends or school vacations.
- Establish trust.
- Teach coping skills.
- Help the student develop vocabulary to express feelings and to vent anger or frustration; help the student recognize the need to communicate.
- Use cognitive-behavioral interventions (e.g., errors in thinking) where there's evidence the student is using negative patterns of thinking and behaving.
- Teach self-affirming behaviors.
- Use play therapy with younger children.
- Know the signs of depression.
- Don't ignore the student or give up on the child but be cautious about encouraging or reinforcing "down" behaviors.
- Provide opportunities for the student to get positive reinforcement from others.
- Identify a person for the student to go to when necessary.

- Prevent other students from bullying; provide a safe environment.
- Identify positively reinforcing activities and increase the student's participation in them.
- Teach relaxation techniques.
- Teach problem solving.
- Teach self-monitoring.
- Don't ignore the student or dismiss student talk of self-harming behavior.
- Teach anger management if the student is displaying aggression.
- Work with student on self-regulation and self-monitoring.
- Maintain routine and foreshadow change so the student doesn't become overwhelmed.
- Change the activity if the student is becoming agitated.
- Teach social skills and social interaction skills and work on social adjustment.
- Encourage the child to do something enjoyable to help the student to refresh and refocus (e.g., physical activity can help alleviate depression—encourage the student to move around, take a walk, etc.).
- Work with the student on developing assertive responses to being victimized.

Summary

Treatment is very effective, and the prognosis for treatment of depression in children is good. Following are reasons for optimism:

- With treatment, episodes are shorter and recovery is quicker.
- Even if episodes recur, recognizing the signs and getting prompt treatment can alleviate their severity.
- Treatment reduces the likelihood of recurrence and/or the severity of the episode.

Students with a diagnosis of depression do not automatically qualify for special education under the Individuals with Disabilities Education Act (IDEA). Keep in mind that IEP teams cannot make DSM-IV diagnoses and physicians cannot identify a child as having special education needs under IDEA. If a student with a mental health diagnosis does not qualify for special education under IDEA, schools may serve these students in their regular education programs or by using a 504 Plan.

Communication with the family and the student's mental health team (physician, therapist, etc.) is critical. It is important for school personnel to know the possible side effects of medications the student is taking, as well as how the disease is manifested for that student.

Flexibility is key to working with students who have a mental illness. Schedules, workloads, expectations, and time lines may need to be adjusted as the student experiences more or fewer symptoms.

Classroom Management for Students With Obsessive Compulsive Disorder (OCD)

Overview

- OCD is one of the anxiety disorders.
- An *obsession* is an uncontrollable idea or emotion; a *compulsion* is a repetitive behavior in response to an obsession. For example, a teenager may be obsessed with cleanliness or have a fear of disease. The student is then compelled to repeatedly wash up or clean. OCD usually involves both obsessions and compulsions, but an individual may have only one or the other.
- With OCD, the brain gets "stuck" on thoughts or urges and cannot let go. The individual feels as though the task *has* to be performed or the thought repeated, and it interferes with everyday life.
- OCD is sometimes comorbid with depression, eating disorders, substance abuse, ADHD, and other anxiety disorders.
- OCD affects approximately 1 in 200 children and adolescents.
- OCD typically begins in adolescence or early childhood; the average age of onset for OCD is 10.2. At least one-third of adult cases began in childhood.
- Males are more likely to develop OCD in childhood; females are more likely to have their first symptoms after age 20.
- The disease appears to be caused by the interaction of neurobiology and environment, including viral infections or environmental

toxins. OCD may develop or worsen after a strep infection. This is known as Pediatric Autoimmune Neuropsychiatric Disorders Associated with Strep (PANDAS). Stressors that can trigger OCD include developmental changes, such as starting school, and significant losses, such as a death or move to a new area.

- OCD tends to run in families, but although having a family history of OCD indicates an individual's disposition toward having the disorder, it does not guarantee it. The family may not be aware of a family history of the illness, because it may have been kept secret and hidden.
- OCD is often underdiagnosed and undertreated. Treatment includes psychotherapy (often cognitive-behavioral therapy) and medications such as serotonin reuptake inhibitors (SSRIs) like Anafranil (clomipramine), Zoloft (sertraline), Prozac (fluoxetine), or Paxil (paroxetine).
- Some children, particularly younger ones, may not recognize they have a problem or may not be willing to admit their behaviors.
- As peer pressure becomes more prominent, an adolescent with OCD may have increased stress and fear as he tries even harder to hide symptoms.
- OCD is not the child's "fault," and the student cannot stop by merely trying harder. Insight into the illness often provides the child with little relief.
- Individuals who suffer from OCD often feel as though they are going crazy.
- Children and adolescents with OCD often do not feel well—this may be due to stress, lack of sleep, poor eating habits, or a combination.
- In children and adolescents, OCD may worsen disruptive behavior, cause attention problems, and interfere with learning.
- Change is stressful for those with OCD, even if the change is for the better.

Symptoms

- Symptoms persist, make no sense, and interfere with day-to-day life
- The disease takes up a great deal of time and produces a high degree of stress or anxiety.
- The child may have an unreasonable fear of illness, germs, and contamination. The student may have chapped hands from constant washing and make frequent trips to the bathroom.

- Homework may have holes from compulsive erasures; the student may spend hours unproductively doing homework. The student may insist on constantly checking or reviewing work. Difficulty completing simple tasks may result in academic difficulties.
- The student may be slow getting ready for bed or getting going in the morning and may experience sleep deprivation because of bedtime rituals.
- Arguing about simple things like table settings or how the closet is arranged
- Being unable to "let go"
- Engaging in outbursts when questioned about odd rituals or desires
- Engaging in self-injurious behavior
- Feeling depression/shame about the symptoms, sometimes resulting in being very secretive (trying to hide symptoms or rituals)
- Having school or social phobia, separation anxiety, or extreme versions of childhood fears (e.g., the bogeyman in the closet or under the bed)
- Having social difficulties, such as withdrawing from friends and activities
- Sexual issues, such as unwanted sexual thoughts, disgust for kissing or hugging for fear of contamination, or compulsive masturbation.
- Common obsessions for children and adolescents include the following:
  - o Fear of causing harm to self or others
  - o Fear of dirt, germs, illness, contamination
  - o Fear of harm coming to self or family
  - o Lucky and unlucky numbers
  - o Need for order and precision
  - o Preoccupation with body wastes
  - o Preoccupation with religious issues (e.g., death, afterlife)
  - o Sexual thoughts

- Common compulsions include the following:
  - o Checking and rechecking to make doors are locked, lights are off, etc.
  - o Cleaning rituals
  - o Grooming rituals, such as showering or hand washing
  - o Hoarding or collecting things
  - o Need for constant reassurance

o Need to do things in a precise order, take a certain route, or check and redo schoolwork
o Need to touch
o Putting objects in specific places or order

- Mornings, evenings, and mealtimes can be especially difficult for children and adolescents with OCD for the following reasons:
  o It usually takes time for them to go through their rituals. They are stressed to get ready and get to school as well as complete their rituals, and the combination makes the stress worse.
  o At meals, there may be fear of contamination or germs; individual may self-restrict diet and refuse to eat what is served.
  o There may also be rituals in the evening for doing homework, getting ready for bed, and so on.
  o Because of these rituals, the child or adolescent may not get enough sleep.

Possible School Interventions

Possible School Interventions for Students With Obsessive-Compulsive Disorder

- Keep in mind that much of the student's attention and working memory may be taken up by obsessions, and there may be little left over for work tasks.
- If the student repeatedly erases and rewrites, tape record work, have the student use a computer, or provide copies of notes or an outline.
- Allow breaks during tests or extra time to complete tests, give untimed tests or oral tests, have student write answers rather than filling in circles, provide a quiet place for taking the test, use letters rather than numbers if numbers are a problem.
- Have flexible time lines for assignments.

- Arrange for appropriate escapes if students need to leave the room. For example, have a private signal students can use if they are becoming overly anxious, seat a child near the door for unobtrusive exits, or seat a child near peers who can ignore repetitive behaviors.
- Keep the number of folders, notebooks, etc. to a minimum.
- Provide extra transition time between classes or activities.
- Be flexible on bathroom breaks, as deciding whether or not to ask may be an additional problem for the student.
- Teach stress management and relaxation techniques.
- Work on increasing self-esteem.

Possible School Interventions for Students With Obsessive-Compulsive Disorder

- Decrease the amount of work—allow student to complete every other problem, for example.
- Break up large amounts of reading or tape record the material.
- Break larger assignments into smaller segments and grade each separately.
- Try to avoid open-ended assignments, such as having the student pick a topic to research, as this may cause additional stress from decision making.
- Adjust homework, because evenings may be a very stressful time.
- Lateness and slowness are issues so let the student know what the parameters of the assignment are (e.g., does spelling count or not), give a time limit, and accept what the student finishes.
- Give the student with OCD materials or paper first (avoid fears of "contamination").
- Provide a separate set of books for at home.
- Cover the material already read or allow the student to use a marker to cross it out to avoid repetition.
- Allow the use of a computer and/or calculator if helpful to the student.
- Redirect the student rather than giving consequences for repetitive behaviors.
- Reward successes but avoid punishing failures.
- Teach social skills: peer relationships are often difficult for students with OCD, as they may be stressed trying to hide their symptoms.
- Help the student identify activities he or she enjoys to ease social situations.
- Identify a "safe" resource person with whom the student can talk when stressed.
- Teach social communication skills.
- If appropriate, use tokens to limit the number of repetitions, bathroom breaks, etc.
- Don't tolerate teasing or bullying by other students.
- Accept work that is not perfect; avoid reinforcing perfectionism.
- Assist the student to deal with change by foreshadowing and trying to keep the schedule as consistent as possible.
- Gradually set time limits for the student.
- Keep in mind that students with OCD may be slow workers but aren't necessarily slow learners.
- Be flexible with scheduling, especially because mornings are stressful for these students. Consider a later start, scheduling high-demand classes for later in the day, and so on.
- Working with the therapist, consider cognitive-behavioral interventions, such as errors in thinking.

Summary

Four Stages of Life With OCD (Chansky, 2000):

1. Noticing that something is going on and help is needed
2. Beginning treatment
3. Midtreatment
4. Maintenance

Although there is no "cure" for OCD and the illness is chronic, it is highly treatable. Treatment may include maintenance to prevent further recurrence once the initial treatment phase has been successful. It is generally harder to get OCD under control than it is to maintain control. Recurrences are normal and, in some cases, predictable.

Students with an obsessive-compulsive disorder diagnosis do not automatically qualify for special education under the Individuals with Disabilities Education Act (IDEA). Keep in mind that IEP (Individualized Education Program) teams cannot make DSM-IV diagnoses and physicians cannot identify a child as having special education needs under IDEA. If a student with a mental health diagnosis does not qualify for special education under IDEA, schools may serve these students in their regular education programs or by using a 504 Plan.

Flexibility is key to working with students who have a mental illness. Schedules, workloads, expectations, and time lines may need to be adjusted as the student experiences more or fewer symptoms.

It is important to work with the family and the student's mental health team to be aware of side effects of medication, as well as how the illness is manifested in this individual.

Classroom Management for Students With Oppositional Defiant Disorder (ODD)

Overview

- Oppositional defiant disorder is an on-going pattern of uncooperative, defiant, and hostile behavior.
- Students with ODD often have a strong need for power and control. Adults tend to focus on the outcome of a disagreement, while children with ODD focus on the process of creating an argument; they "push your buttons" to gain a feeling of control.

- ODD is often comorbid with ADHD, mood disorders, anxiety disorder, and/or learning disabilities. Studies show that 40–65 percent of children with ADHD also have ODD.
- Some children with ODD may develop a conduct disorder (CD). ODD and CD are strongly related but clearly different. Age of onset for ODD is earlier than for CD. Most adolescents with CD have a history of ODD, but not all those with ODD develop CD.
- Causes are not known, but theories include an inherited predisposition, chemical imbalances in the brain, and the child's temperament coupled with environmental factors such as the family's response to the temperament.
- Many parents report that their child with ODD was more rigid and demanding from an early age than other children.
- It is estimated that 5 percent of all school-age children have ODD.
- ODD usually begins by age 8 and not later than early adolescence.
- ODD is more common in boys before puberty; after puberty, the ratio of boys to girls evens out.
- Treatment usually includes therapy and medications for comorbid conditions. If those interventions fail, then medications such as atypical antipsychotics (Risperidal [risperidone], Zyprexa [olanzapine]), mood stabilizers (lithium, Epival [divalproex sodium]), and others (clonidine) may be used.
- Everyone involved with the child must react consistently. It is important for parents and school staff to communicate frequently so that the student cannot play one against the other.
- Students with ODD have many behaviors of concern. It is important to prioritize what to target, what to "live with," and what to ignore for the time being.
- It is important to help the student save face and maintain dignity.
- Children with ODD are rarely truly sorry, and forcing them to apologize sets up yet another power struggle.

Symptoms

- Active defiance and refusal to comply with adult requests and rules
- Blaming others for own mistakes
- Deliberate attempts to annoy or upset people
- Easily annoyed by others; touchy
- Excessive arguing with adults
- Frequent temper tantrums
- Frequently angry and resentful

- Given praise, destroying or sabotaging own efforts
- Saying mean, hateful things when upset; spiteful and vindictive
- Diagnosis is based on the following criteria:
  - Behavior occurs more frequently than is typical of others of comparable age and developmental level.
  - Causes significant impairment in social, academic, or occupational functioning.
  - Pattern lasts at least six months, during which four or more of the characteristics are displayed.
  - Criteria for conduct disorder are not met; if individual is 18 or older, criteria for antisocial personality disorder are not met.

- Children with ODD have the following thought patterns:
  - They believe others must treat them fairly, even if they are not fair in return.
  - They believe they can defeat adult authority figures.
  - They believe they can outlast authority figures.
  - They fail to learn from experience.
  - They have at least some hope of winning, which encourages them to continue to take adults on.
  - They need to feel tough.
  - They seek revenge when angered.

- Children and adolescents with ODD may behave as follows:
  - Are very controlling
  - Blame others for causing own misbehavior
  - Deal with failure, stress, frustration through ODD behavior as a way of being "in control."
  - Deny responsibility for own behavior
  - Seem stuck on no
  - Try to play people off others
  - View things as all-or-nothing or clearly black-and-white

Possible School Interventions

Possible School Interventions for Students With Oppositional Defiant Disorder

• Make sure all adults working with the student know how to interact effectively with the student.	• Teach social skills, anger management skills, and classroom skills (how to be a student).
• Use controlled choices: "You can do A or you can do B."	• Work on helping the child be more flexible and improve frustration tolerance; teach calming techniques.

Possible School Interventions for Students With Oppositional Defiant Disorder

- Speak in a calm, emotionless voice. You may have to sound like a broken record.
- Be very cautious about accepting information from the student about what others have done/not done.
- Use positive reinforcement and positive feedback, but be aware that this approach may be problematic if overdone so that the student becomes more oppositional.
- Use indirect reinforcement: whisper to the student, use notes, provide rewards without direct interaction or feedback, walk past the student giving a quick comment without eye contact or giving the student an opportunity for confrontation.
- Refer control from yourself: blame the schedule, the program, or the rules.
- Include physical activities so the student can release pent-up energy.
- Don't try to talk when the student is being oppositional; instead, wait until you can be alone with the student, the student is in a relatively good mood, and tension is low.
- Teach replacement behaviors; be sure the student knows what to do "instead."

- Allow self-timeouts to prevent overreactions.
- Pick your battles; avoid power struggles and arguing; disengage.
- Deflect arguing: "Nevertheless, here is what must happen."
- Have clear rules and consequences; be specific about behavior and avoid generalizations such as "be good."
- Keep consequences fair, reasonable, and progressive.
- Use a behavior contract that includes the expectation, the consequence, and the reward for compliance.
- Conduct an FBA to help determine triggers/antecedents, as well as maintaining consequences. This includes developing a hypothesis as to whether the behavior is symptomatic, learned, or a combination. Observe the student; gather anecdotal information; and interview teachers, other staff, parents, the student (if appropriate), and the therapist. Then develop a behavior plan that can be tested to see if the behavior can be modified.
- Have a consistent daily schedule.
- Have older children keep a journal to help them identify trigger events and emotional cycles.

(Continued)

(Continued)

Possible School Interventions for Students With Oppositional Defiant Disorder

- Consider cognitive-behavioral interventions such as errors in thinking.
- Have a warning system; for example, 1-2-3, three strikes, warning card, stoplight (red, yellow, green), or hourglass.
- Have clear rules and expectations that are not open for discussion.
- Consider a points/levels system.
- Prepare a script for yourself to help avoid being drawn into an argument.
- Modify the environment (seating, physical comfort, group size, noise, reasonable expectations).

- Avoid being overly restrictive and "tightening the screws"; keep in mind that harshness increases the student's negative feelings, which may intensify the need to "get even." Putting a student with ODD in his or her "place" models the behavior we are trying to modify.
- Foreshadow change.

Summary

- Life may not be easy for children and adolescents with ODD, but with treatment, reasonable adjustments can be made so that life may be *easier*.
- James Chandler (see resource list below) suggests three main paths that children and adolescents with ODD follow:
  1. Some seem to outgrow the symptoms and behaviors.

  2. Some develop a conduct disorder.

  3. Some continue to have ODD either with or without comorbid conditions.

Students with an oppositional defiant disorder diagnosis do not automatically qualify for special education under the Individuals with Disabilities Education Act (IDEA). Keep in mind that IEP (Individualized

Education Program) teams cannot make DSM-IV diagnoses and physicians cannot identify a child as having special education needs under IDEA. If a student with a mental health diagnosis does not qualify for special education under IDEA, schools may serve these students in their regular education programs or by using a 504 Plan.

Communication with the family and the student's mental health team (physician, therapist, etc.) is critical. It is important for school personnel to know the possible side effects of medications the student is taking, as well as how the disease is manifested for that student.

Flexibility is key to working with students who have a mental illness. Schedules, workloads, expectations, and time lines may need to be adjusted as the student experiences more or fewer symptoms.

Classroom Management for Students With Posttraumatic Stress Disorder (PTSD)

Overview

- PTSD has sometimes been called "shell shock" or "battle fatigue," because it was first identified in combat veterans.
- World Health Organization (2007) definition of PTSD: "A delayed or protracted response to a stressful event or situation (of either brief or long duration) of an exceptionally threatening or catastrophic nature, which is likely to cause pervasive distress in almost anyone" (F43.1).
- PTSD is an anxiety disorder that develops after a traumatic event or ordeal. It typically appears within three months of the event; however, symptoms may not appear until years later. PTSD is diagnosed if symptoms are apparent at least one month after the ordeal.
- PTSD is commonly comorbid with depression, substance abuse, other anxiety disorders, ADHD, oppositional defiant disorder, conduct disorder, and phobias.
- *Trauma* is often defined as an experience that is emotionally painful, distressful, or shocking. Physical traumas and emotional traumas, natural disasters and manmade disasters, can all lead to PTSD.
- Traumatic events for children and adolescents that may result in PTSD commonly include sexual abuse or assault, physical

abuse or assault, being the victim of a violent crime, being in an automobile accident, being in a disaster such as a fire or tornado, being in an event where there was a fear of death, being attacked by a dog, or witnessing such traumas (violence in the home, murder, etc.).

- Risk factors include a previous history of depression, history of physical or sexual abuse, family history of anxiety, dysfunctional family, alcohol or drug abuse, and separation from family at an early age.

- Relevant factors in the development of PTSD include the child's age and developmental level when the trauma occurs, the type and severity of the trauma, the level of support from the parents, the proximity of the child to the event, and the psychiatric condition of the parents or caregivers.

- There is no evidence of a direct biological predisposition to PTSD.

- One percent of the general population is said to have experienced an event that might result in a diagnosis of PTSD.

- Studies reported by the National Center for PTSD indicate that 15–43 percent of girls and 14–43 percent of boys have experienced at least one traumatic event in their lifetimes; of those who have, 3–15 percent of girls and 1–6 percent of boys could be diagnosed with PTSD.

- Treatment includes behavior therapies and medications such as tranquilizers or selective serotonin reuptake inhibitors (SSRIs) such as Prozac (fluoxetine), Zoloft (sertraline), or Paxil (paroxetine).

- Children and adolescents with PTSD are more likely than other students to need remedial assistance in school and are more likely to be suspended from school.

- Children and adolescents may develop psychotic symptoms, have thoughts of suicide, and have a high rate of psychiatric hospitalization. Inappropriate sexual behavior and behaviors such as lying, stealing, and truancy are common.

- PTSD is often a chronic disorder: more than 40 percent of children still suffer symptoms one year after diagnosis.

Symptoms

Symptoms of PTSD in children and adolescents can vary greatly, and the illness is often misdiagnosed. Symptoms, which can last from several months to many years, include the following:

- Agitation
- Denial or repression of the trauma
- Difficulty with declarative memory (recalling lists or facts) or fragmented memory and dissociative amnesia
- Disorganization
- Distress on anniversaries of the trauma
- Efforts to avoid feelings, thoughts, and activities associated with the event
- Excessive use of alcohol or other drugs to self-medicate and "escape"
- Fear of one's life being threatened or taken
- Feelings of detachment or estrangement; inability to feel lovingly toward others
- Flashbacks (can be emotions, sounds, smells, mental images)
- Guilt that the event was one's own fault; survivor guilt if family or friends did not survive
- Hopelessness about the future
- Hypersensitivity with two or more of the following: sleep disturbances, anger or explosiveness, sudden irritability, difficulty concentrating, exaggerated responses to noise or when startled, physical reactions (rapid heart rate, rapid breathing, nausea, etc.) to situations that recall the trauma
- Intense vigilance
- Nervousness when people get too close physically
- Nightmares and/or sleeplessness
- Preoccupation with danger
- Re-enacting, retelling, and drawing that may appear compulsive but does not reduce the individual's anxiety about the trauma
- Replaying the incident over and over again in one's mind
- Withdrawal, flat affect

Age-Specific Features of PTSD

Age	Features
Very young children (5 or younger)	Few symptoms reported because of the need for verbal descriptions (young children don't have the necessary abstract thinking skills and/or vocabulary to describe their trauma)

(Continued)

(Continued)

Age	Features
	More generalized fears and anxieties
	Trembling, immobility
	Separation anxiety
	Sleep disturbances
	Regression (e.g., thumb sucking) or loss of a previously acquired skill such as toilet training
	Posttraumatic play that recreates the trauma or general themes of the trauma
Elementary age children (ages 6–11)	When recalling the traumatic event, putting events in the wrong order
	Being hyperalert to stimuli perceived as warning signs or danger signals
	Extreme withdrawal
	Acting out, disruption
	Problems attending to tasks, concentrating
	Regression
	Irrational fears
	School refusal, school phobia
	Flat affect
	Anger, fighting
	Physical complaints (headache, stomachache)
	Re-enacting the trauma through play, drawings, or words
Adolescent (ages 12–17)	More closely resembles adult PTSD
	Suicidal thoughts
	Guilt
	Revenge fantasies
	Flashbacks
	Depression, numb emotions, flat affect
	Substance abuse
	Peer problems such as alienation or withdrawal
	Antisocial behavior, acting out
	Posttraumatic re-enactment
	Impulsivity and aggression

Possible School Interventions

Possible School Interventions for Students With Posttraumatic Stress Disorder

- Be flexible with routines to allow for symptoms such as sleeplessness; a routine can be helpful in restoring a sense of normalcy, but don't force it.
- Teach coping and relaxation skills.
- Accept the child's behaviors while encouraging and reinforcing more appropriate behaviors.
- Listen but don't force a student to talk.
- Reassure the student—"You're safe," and "It was not your fault." Reassurance is critical.
- Avoid criticizing the regressive behavior, fears, etc. or shaming the student.
- Allow the student choices and work on decision-making skills so that the student feels a sense of control.
- Provide support for routine tasks, even those may be "too much" at times.
- Let the student know the reaction to trauma is normal.
- Allow the student to be sad; don't force him to "get tough."
- Teach stress management techniques.
- Teach social skills so student can feel comfortable interacting with others.
- Be aware of cultural differences in dealing with trauma and its aftermath.
- If the trauma happened at school or in the community, allow students to opt out of discussions.
- Use cognitive-behavioral interventions, such as errors in thinking, to challenge self-damaging thoughts.
- Provide a calm, safe place to go and someone for the student to talk with when symptoms occur.
- Provide a safe, supportive environment for the student.
- Learn what might trigger symptoms for the student and try to avoid or prevent those situations.
- Maintain personal distance from the child; be cautious about touching the child.

Summary

- There are four categories of symptoms: intrusive (flashbacks, nightmares), avoidant (avoiding reminders, severing associations with others), hyperarousal (anger, irritability, disorganization, jumpiness), and associative (use of alcohol or other drugs).
- Symptoms may last for weeks or months but often decrease over time.

- PTSD may recur spontaneously.
- If untreated, PTSD can become a chronic condition; however, counseling soon after the trauma can reduce some of the symptoms.
- PTSD is often accompanied by depression, and the depression must also be treated.
- Children's brains are physically affected by extreme stress—the hippocampus, which processes memory, may actually be changed.
- The mnemonic DREAMS may be useful for screening for PTSD

    Detachment

    Re-experiencing the event

    Event had emotional effects

    Avoidance

    Month in duration

    Sympathetic hyperactivity or hypervigilance

Students with a posttramatic stress disorder diagnosis do not automatically qualify for special education under the Individuals with Disabilities Education Act (IDEA). Keep in mind that IEP teams cannot make DSM-IV diagnoses and physicians cannot identify a child as having special education needs under IDEA. If a student with a mental health diagnosis does not qualify for special education under IDEA, schools may serve these students in their regular education programs or by using a 504 Plan.

Communication with the family and the student's mental health team (physician, therapist, etc.) is critical. It is important for school personnel to know the possible side effects of medications the student is taking, as well as how the disease is manifested for that individual.

Flexibility is key to working with students who have a mental illness. Schedules, workloads, expectations, and time lines may need to be adjusted as the student experiences more or fewer symptoms.

Classroom Management for Students With Reactive Attachment Disorder (RAD)

Overview

- RAD, an inappropriate ability to relate to peers and adults in most settings, begins when children are unable to attach to a primary caregiver during the first two years of life and this lack negatively impacts their relationships. RAD manifests itself before age five, and the problems may continue as the child grows older.

- There are two types of RAD: inhibited (failure to initiate or respond socially) and disinhibited (excessive familiarity with strangers).

- RAD is not solely explained by a developmental delay or pervasive developmental disorder (PDD).

- The causes of RAD are not known. Most children with RAD had severe problems in their early years, such as physical or emotional abuse or neglect, inadequate care in an out-of-home placement, or multiple or traumatic losses or changes in their primary caregiver. RAD is common in foster and adopted children but also occurs in children where, at an early age, there was a divorce, illness, or death.

- Factors that put a child at high risk are sudden separation from the primary caretaker, frequent moves and placements, prenatal exposure to alcohol/other drugs, and unprepared parents with poor parenting skills.

- Students with RAD will not outgrow it, and treatment is critical.

- Behavior usually gets worse before it gets better, so support the parents and work with the mental health team. If school is "on hold" while other therapy issues are addressed, try at least to maintain the status quo and not make the problems worse.

- The most important thing you can do for the student with RAD is to create a safe environment.

- A student with RAD manipulates to control a world he considers unsafe and even fatal. The battle for control is constant.

- The separation process for children with RAD has three stages: initial protests (crying, screaming, etc.), depression (withdrawal), and anger or detachment.

- A student with RAD is reinforced when adults "lose it."

- Students with RAD may make false accusations of abuse against parents, school staff, or other caregivers. They may pretend to be fearful of their parents to reinforce the false allegations.

- Students with RAD often try to triangulate (separate, play one off the other) parents and school personnel. Good communication with the parents is critical. Set up an alternative communication system with the parents (e.g., phone, e-mail, written information sent to work address or a relative's home), because the student may destroy notes or fail to bring papers home.

- Timeouts do not work with students with RAD, because they want to be isolated.

- Adolescents with RAD are often part of the juvenile justice system.

Symptoms

- Acting superficial and phony
- Being bossy
- Being fascinated by gore, evil, destruction, etc.
- Being manipulative
- Being overly friendly to strangers but unable to be affectionate with those who are close
- Blaming others; not accepting responsibility for own actions
- Dealing with stress by banging head; scratching, biting or cutting self; or rocking back and forth
- Engaging in abnormal eating, either gorging or starving
- Engaging in regressive behaviors (babytalk, noisemaking, animal noises, etc.)
- Generally having no friends; considered too controlling or bossy by other children
- Having difficulty understanding how one's behavior affects others; lack of empathy
- Having difficulty with cause-and-effect
- Having mood swings
- Having poor impulse control
- Jabbering and speaking nonsensically, slurring words, or mumbling
- Lack of guilt or remorse
- Making poor eye contact unless lying (in which case they usually make good eye contact)
- Often giving "stiff" hugs; not being "cuddly"
- Often preferring to be alone and not doing well in groups
- Refusing to do assignments or doing them poorly
- Sexual acting out
- Showing physical aggression, including injuring animals or other people, usually with a lack of remorse afterward
- Stealing, chronic lying
- Throwing temper tantrums
- Viewing the world as unsafe and untrustworthy

Possible School Interventions

Possible School Interventions for Students With Reactive Adjustment Disorder

• Keep a predictable schedule and routine so that the student gets the message that you are trustworthy.	• Teach social skills by modeling; explain "why" certain behaviors are desireable/undesireable.
• Avoid power struggles; be matter of fact; choose your battles.	• Teach relaxation and stress reduction.

Possible School Interventions for Students With Reactive Adjustment Disorder

- Make information relevant and meaningful to the child. The student is focused on being safe, so will typically not engage in learning unless it is seen as relevant to the student's immediate needs or long-term survival.
- Students with RAD usually need immediate feedback and gratification. They have difficulty dealing with delayed consequences.
- Allow choices: reinforce the idea that the student continually makes choices, then move to making "better" choices.
- Build self-esteem in the student.
- Insist on eye contact.
- Avoid harsh, punitive consequences, as those will only reinforce the student's mistrust of adults.
- Standard rewards don't work (stickers, treats, etc.).
- Use a team approach: one person should not be responsible alone.
- Reinforce that you (the teacher) are in charge. Have the student repeat that ("Yes, Mrs. Smith, you are the boss."), but don't be sarcastic or argumentative. Insist on the use of titles to reinforce rank (Mrs. Smith, Coach Jones).
- Record assignments for the student if he has difficulty remembering them.
- If the student is at a point in therapy where it is appropriate, work on social skills and group skills.
- Try to avoid group activities, as this may increase the child's anxiety and need to control.
- Keep in mind that regardless of the number of times you have helped the student, tomorrow you may be the enemy and the student will not recall your helpfulness.
- Choose your battles.
- Provide movement activities such as dancing, rhythmic movement, or sitting in a rocking chair.
- Acknowledge good decisions and behavior; give matter-of-fact consequences for inappropriate behavior or poor decisions.
- Do not accept slurred speech; instead ignore it (but be sure the student knows the acceptable response).
- Be consistent and specific. Do not cut the student any "slack," as it will probably be viewed as room to manipulate or try to regain control.
- Avoid being alone with the student (you want to avoid false accusations).
- Use natural consequences when possible ("You made a mess. Clean it up.").
- Have a crisis plan, including a place the student can go to regain control if need be.
- If the student is stressed, try to determine if he is bored or overwhelmed and adjust accordingly.

Summary

Treatment of RAD is challenging and difficult. Keep the following in mind:

- Close collaboration between the family and mental health professionals is critical for a successful future.

- It takes a great deal of work and time for treatment to be successful. Therefore, parents may not have the energy to focus on anything else for the time being. School staff should support and respect that.

Students with a reactive attachment disorder diagnosis do not automatically qualify for special education under the Individuals with Disabilities Education Act (IDEA). Keep in mind that IEP (Individualized Education Program) teams cannot make DSM-IV diagnoses and physicians cannot identify a child as having special education needs under IDEA. If a student with a mental health diagnosis does not qualify for special education under IDEA, schools may serve these students in their regular education programs or by using a 504 Plan.

Communication with the family and the student's mental health team (physician, therapist, etc.) is critical. It is important for school personnel to know the possible side effects of medications the student is taking, as well as how the disease is manifested for that student.

Flexibility is key to working with students who have a mental illness. Schedules, workloads, expectations, and time lines may need to be adjusted as the student experiences more or fewer symptoms.

Classroom Management for Students With Schizophrenia

Overview

- Schizophrenia is a profound disruption in cognition and emotion and affects the student in interpersonal relationships, self-care, academic achievement, and/or work skills. Schizophrenia is not just one symptom but a pattern of observable signs and symptoms. These symptoms persist for at least one month and do not appear until a child is at least seven years old.
- *Delusions* are strongly held false beliefs, which the individual holds onto despite evidence to the contrary.
- *Hallucinations* can be visual (seeing things that are not there), auditory (hearing voices that others cannot hear), tactile (feeling things that others don't or feeling something touching the skin when there is nothing there), olfactory (smelling things that others cannot or not smelling the same things others do), and gustatory (tasting things that aren't there). Auditory hallucinations or "voices" may be positive, negative, reassuring, or neutral. The most common are threatening, punitive, and/or commanding.

- *Psychosis* is a term used to describe psychotic symptoms; schizophrenia is a kind of psychosis. Some psychoses that are not schizophrenia include brain lesions from head traumas or strokes.
- Types of schizophrenia include paranoid schizophrenia (suspicious of others, strong feelings of persecution, delusions, hallucinations) and disorganized schizophrenia (verbally incoherent with moods not appropriate to situations, generally no hallucinations). Paranoid schizophrenia is the most common form. It is especially common in younger males.
- Symptoms of schizophrenia can be mistaken for those of bipolar disorder or depression. Schizophrenia is often comorbid with conduct disorders, learning disabilities, and mental retardation. Schizophrenia is distinguished from autism by the persistence of hallucinations and delusions for at least six months and by the later age of onset (seven or older for schizophrenia, while autism is usually apparent by age three). If there is a history of autism or pervasive developmental disorder (PDD), the additional diagnosis of schizophrenia is only made if prominent delusions or hallucinations are also present.
- Schizophrenia appears to have neurodevelopmental roots—a combination of brain changes, biochemistry, genetic and environmental factors.
- For those children with a genetic predisposition to schizophrenia, the risk of becoming schizophrenic may be as much as 800 percent higher if they come from high-stress, dysfunctional families.
- There is disagreement about whether the use of street drugs can trigger schizophrenia. Some sources report that it does. For example, psychiatrists in inner-city areas report that use of marijuana is a factor in up to 80 percent of schizophrenia cases. Researchers in New Zealand found that those who used marijuana by age 15 were three times more likely to develop illnesses such as schizophrenia. Others report that symptoms resulting from the use of street drugs may mimic schizophrenia but the individual is not truly schizophrenic.
- Schizophrenia is much rarer in children than in adults: estimates range from 1–2 in 10,000 to 1 in 40,000 children have the disease versus 1 in 100 adults. Children with schizophrenia have more pronounced neurological abnormalities than do adults with schizophrenia.
- Of children with schizophrenia, 80 percent have auditory hallucinations; 50 percent have delusions.

- Schizophrenia tends to begin at an earlier age in men/boys than in women/girls. Males generally begin showing signs between ages 15 and 20; females generally begin to show signs between ages 20 to 25. Females develop schizophrenia at a rate of about 50–75 percent that of males. Males are less responsive to medication than females, and the long-term outcome tends to be worse for men than for women.
- Those with schizophrenia have a difficult time understanding that they are ill, because the part of the brain affected by schizophrenia is often the same part responsible for self-analysis.
- The long-term outlook is worse if the individual has poor social supports, a strong family history of schizophrenia, the illness came on slowly, and/or treatment was delayed.

Symptoms

Early Warning Signs in Youngsters With Schizophrenia

- Behaving like a younger child
- Being suspicious of others
- Confused thinking
- Delays in language and other functions long before psychotic symptoms occur
- Experiencing a change in behavior and/or personality
- Extreme moodiness
- Hallucinations—seeing things and hearing voices that are not real
- Having a hard time differentiating fantasy or dreams from reality
- Having difficulty relating to peers and keeping friends
- Hyperactivity or lethargia
- Inappropriate responses, such as laughing or crying at inappropriate times
- Severe anxiety or fearfulness
- Sleep problems
- Stating or believing that others are "out to get me"
- Talking about strange fears and ideas
- Unusual or bizarre thoughts and ideas
- Withdrawal and increasing isolation

Positive Symptoms: Those That Reflect an Excess or Abnormal Distortion of Normal Functions

- Catatonic behavior (motionless with apparent unawareness, rigid or bizarre posture, aimless and excessive motor activity, marked decrease in reaction to the surroundings)

- Delusions
- Disorganized speech/thinking
- Grossly disorganized behavior
- Hallucinations

Negative Symptoms: A Diminishing or Loss of Normal Functions

- Deterioration in personal hygiene; very poor personal hygiene
- Difficulty making or keeping friends; not wanting friends
- Difficulty or inability to speak (alogia)
- Flattening of the affect
- Inappropriate social skills or lack of interest in socializing
- Lack of emotion
- Lack of interest in life
- Low energy
- No motivation
- Social isolation

Cognitive Symptoms

- Difficulty expressing thoughts
- Difficulty integrating thoughts, feelings, and behavior
- Difficulty understanding
- Disorganized thinking
- Poor concentration
- Poor memory
- Slow thinking

Possible School Interventions

Possible School Interventions for Students With Schizophrenia

- If the student has disordered thinking, help to sort out what is relevant and what is not. Teach planning skills. Write things down and make sure the student is aware of expectations. Clarify the "bottom line" and try to keep things simple and concrete.
- Be flexible, as symptoms may come and go, even on a daily basis.

- Help the student set reasonable goals.
- Be accepting, caring, and supportive; provide a safe environment for the student.
- Many students with schizophrenia have difficulty concentrating and are easily distracted. Break tasks down into smaller pieces, minimize distractions, and have a plan to redirect the student to return to the task at hand.

(Continued)

(Continued)

Possible School Interventions for Students With Schizophrenia

- Teach social skills, including language skills related to interpersonal interactions. Allow time for role-playing and feedback. Develop scripts with the student if necessary.
- Use cognitive-behavioral interventions.
- Have additional materials, books, and supplies available for the student to use if the student doesn't bring them.
- If there are language issues, including social or pragmatic language issues, consider involving the speech/language pathologist. Materials such as those developed by Michelle Garcia Winner (www.socialthinking.com) may be helpful for classroom use.
- Try to keep stress low, as the student may run if overstressed.
- Allow extra time and/or modify assignments if the student seems to be working slowly.
- Explore various recreational activities so that the student has something to do with leisure time besides watch TV.
- Go slowly with new materials, skills, and concepts.
- Have a crisis plan; consider physical restraint if the student becomes dangerous to self or others.
- Give short, concise directions.
- Have a written schedule and maintain structure, routine, and predictability.

- Assist the student with planning and organizational skills.
- If there are mild neurological signs, such as poor motor skills or difficulty differentiating "left" from "right," alert the physical education teacher and others of the potential impact on performance. If there are motor abnormalities, consider involving the physical therapist (PT) and/or occupational therapist (OT).
- Work with the student to relieve anxiety and have a plan if the student does become overly anxious.
- Look for ways to motivate the student to become involved in classroom tasks and activities, including work completion and social interactions.
- If the student is hallucinating, don't say that there's "nothing there"—to the student, there *is* something there. Work with the student to provide support for acceptable behavior when hallucinations happen.
- Support a healthy lifestyle for the student, including proper diet, exercise, and enough rest/sleep.
- Keep an anecdotal record of changes and bizarre actions/words/writing; be aware of relapse signs.
- Socializing may be exhausting for this student—he may have difficulty with groups or when everyone is excited—so plan accordingly.
- Try to avoid sensory overload.

Summary

The more patients and family members understand the disease, the better the treatment and long-term outcome for people with schizophrenia. Following are some concepts that are important to keep in mind:

- The worst approach is to do nothing and hope the disease will go away.
- Many children can be helped with antipsychotic medications and therapy.
- Misconceptions about schizophrenia include the following:
  o It is a multiple personality disorder—not true.
  o People who are schizophrenic are a higher risk for being violent criminals—not true.
  o Schizophrenia is caused by bad parenting or character flaws—not true.

- According to www.netdoctor.co.uk, about one-fourth of people with schizophrenia have one episode, make a good recovery, and have no further problems. Another one-fourth develop a chronic, long-term illness with no remissions. One-half have a long-term illness that comes and goes.

Students with a diagnosis of schizophrenia do not automatically qualify for special education under the Individuals with Disabilities Education Act (IDEA). Keep in mind that IEP (Individualized Education Program) teams cannot make DSM-IV diagnoses and physicians cannot identify a child as having special education needs under IDEA. If a student with a mental health diagnosis does not qualify for special education under IDEA, schools may serve these students in their regular education programs or by using a 504 Plan.

Communication with the family and the student's mental health team (physician, therapist, etc.) is critical. It is important for school personnel to know the possible side effects of medications the student is taking, as well as how the disease is manifested for that student.

Flexibility is key to working with students who have a mental illness. Schedules, workloads, expectations, and time lines may need to be adjusted as the student experiences more or fewer symptoms.

Glossary

Active listening.   Listening attentively to what is being said and then repeating, in the listener's own words, what the listener thinks the speaker said. The listener might use phrases such as "I heard you say ..." or "Is it fair to say you ..." The listener does not have to agree—it's enough for the speaker to feel heard.

Antiseptic bouncing.   Sending the student out of the room on a task or errand. You may want to set up some "errands" with the office (you need some classroom supplies, a Band-Aid, etc.) in the event that you don't have a "real" errand but want to give the student an opportunity to move, get out of the room temporarily, get some attention for appropriately completing the errand, and so on. This also gives you a chance to get the rest of the class working, and they are less likely to respond to inappropriate behavior when the target student returns. You can then work with the target student when he returns and get him caught up and working.

Bibliotherapy.   Using literature to teach problem solving, coping skills, social skills, perspective taking, and so on.

Behavior contracting.   Contracting with the student so that the student completes something the teacher wants done and the student is then rewarded. Contracts can be verbal or written and should be positive. The student should show an accomplishment (e.g., complete a task, participate in an activity, remain outside for recess without fighting, solve a problem positively rather than by fighting). Writing a contract can also help teach a student negotiating skills. Be sure that the student has a reasonable chance of meeting the contract terms.

Classroom meetings.   An opportunity for teachers and students to discuss mutual concerns and solutions. The tone of the meeting is always positive, and there are ground rules to be followed (turn taking, acceptable language, etc.). The idea is to reach a conclusion, not to keep discussing the same topic over and over.

Comic book conversations. Using word and thought bubbles and colors for emotions to help students identify the thoughts and feelings of people having a conversation. (See www.thegraycenter.org.)

Cooperative learning. Learning teams of students that work together. Key features include division of labor, assignment of roles to students, face-to-face interaction, and interdependence wherein all student tasks are necessary for task completion. (See www.cooplearn.org.)

Direct instruction. Using a highly structured instructional approach geared to teaching the specific skills the student lacks. The teacher uses telling, showing, modeling, demonstrating, and prompting to get active responses from students. It is focused on teacher-directed instruction more than on independent seatwork.

Double dipping. Using bibliotherapy to teach both academics and social skills; for example, using war or world conflict to discuss problem-solving skills or compromise.

Empathy, teaching. See *Perspective taking* below.

Engineered choices. Giving the student choices or structured options that are acceptable to both the student and the teacher.

Errors in thinking (good thinking, changing thinking). Based on the premise that students may exhibit patterns of negative thinking and that they must change the way they think to change the way they act, this type of intervention focuses on the idea that thought can control actions; students have the ability to control and change their negative, self-defeating thinking; and students can be taught how to do this and be reinforced for their efforts. For example, a student may give up easily on a task, thinking, "I can't do this—I'm too stupid." The goal is to point out the error in thinking ("You can do this.") and help the student to try again. Another example of a thinking error is failing to take responsibility for one's own behavior: "It wasn't my fault—they made me."

Feedback loop. Providing the student with an example of the behavior and describing the impact it had on the student and/or others, then asking the student if the outcome was what was intended. If the response is no, then the teacher discusses more appropriate alternatives with the student. If the response is yes, the teacher should let it go without argument—the student may be saying yes to cover up or appear tough, but your point has been made.

Foreshadowing.   Telling students what will happen next, or at a certain time; for example, "When the bell rings, we will be going to the music room," or, "Tomorrow there will be a different schedule because . . . and here is what will happen."

Group contingency.   Group reinforcement that is contingent on individual student behavior or group behavior. The entire group is reinforced or not reinforced.

Hero system.   A behavior management approach in which a child's appropriate behavior and/or improvement in behavior results in a reward being given to the entire group/class. The student is then viewed as a "hero" to peers.

Hurdle help.   Providing the student with the help needed to get through or past a difficult situation. The student may not understand the directions or may get stuck on one of the steps of the problem or assignment. Helping the student understand what is supposed to be done, or working with the student to get over the hurdle, may help to avoid escalating a disruptive behavior.

I messages.   Stating feelings or directions in an *I* or *we* format. The goal is to avoid using *you*, which can cause students to be defensive. For example, instead of saying, "You must be quiet," you could say, "We all need to be able to hear the instructions." The purpose is to tell the student what to do (rather than what not to do) and avoid being accusatory. Another example would be to say, "I feel bad when I hear that word. Please use _____ instead."

Ignoring.   If the behavior is relatively minor and will not escalate or spread to other students, ignoring it may be best to avoid reinforcing misbehavior. Knowing what to ignore often is a result of experience with the student who is misbehaving—a process of trial and error. What happens if you ignore the behavior—does it get worse as the student pushes for attention? Does the behavior go away on its own? Do other students get hooked into the behavior so that you now have a larger problem to address?

Modeling.   Acting in a way that you want the student to imitate; using other students as role models for appropriate behavior.

Movement breaks.   An opportunity for a student to stand up, move, stretch, wiggle, etc. in an acceptable manner and without distracting or interrupting other students.

Peer mediation.   A process of conflict resolution that involves trained student mediators, who use a structured process to meet with peers in conflict and try to help resolve the differences. The process is about learning to get along, not about winning and losing. It is not appropriate when criminal activities are involved. (See www .schoolmediationcenter.org.)

Perspective taking/Teaching empathy. Putting yourself in someone else's shoes—how would you feel if the tables were turned? Helping students understand that their behavior impacts others and how. It is often easier to teach empathy using examples (movie clips, TV shows, other scenarios, stories) to minimize student defensiveness. Service learning (see below) is a useful tool, as is restorative justice (also see below) and "I messages" ("I feel frustrated when . . .").

Preteaching. Making certain the student knows the expectations and teaching the student how to meet those expectations before holding the student accountable. For example, a teacher might say, "When it is 'study time,' you are to be in your seat, quiet, and working on unfinished assignments or reading silently."

Power struggles. A battle of wills that typically results in a win/lose situation; for example, "Oh, yes, you will!—Oh, no, I won't!"

Response cost. Loss of tokens or points earned in a token economy (see below) for misbehavior. This is set up as part of the system, and the students are aware of the potential cost ahead of time. Be cautious if the points/tokens aren't meaningful to the students. The students should not be allowed to dig themselves into a hole they cannot get out of in a reasonable manner or time.

Restorative justice. A response to misbehavior that focuses on identifying and repairing the harm done. For example, the student might clean up the mess that was made or work off damage done to materials or equipment. (See www.restorativejustice.com.)

Sensory integration. The brain organizes sensory input (sight, hearing, touch, taste, smell) so that the person can function. If all of that sensory information is not interpreted correctly, a student will experience problems. These might include being overly sensitive to sound or touch, an unusually high or low level of activity, poor coordination, or poor organizational skills. There are different activities for different outcomes (arousal, relaxation, etc.). Consult the occupational therapists (OTs) in your building or district for more information.

Sensory breaks (for arousal and for relaxation). Time for activities that help the student focus and participate. These activities may be done with a therapist or teacher or may be things the student can do him- or herself such as using a small "fidget toy" to help maintain attention, moving rhythmically from one activity to another, having a water bottle or something to chew on, and so on.

Service learning. Combines service activities with learning objectives so that both the server and the recipient benefit. Service learning helps the student to learn empathy/perspective taking. (See www.servicelearning.org.)

Social skills. Behavioral skills that allow students to interact more appropriately and productively with others and to cope with social situations. Students may not have been taught appropriate behavior, may have difficulty reading social cues or dealing with unexpected situations, or may experience discomfort when displaying a certain behavior. In addition to teaching the behaviors, effective social skill instruction includes role-playing and opportunities for the student to practice (with feedback) and generalize the behavior to a variety of settings.

Social stories. A short story that describes a situation, concept, or social skill. Originally developed for students with autism spectrum disorders by Carol Gray, social stories are also sometimes used with children with emotional behavioral disorders and cognitive disabilities. (See www.thegraycenter.org.)

Team building. Activities that promote cooperation, trust, and teamwork with a group, making the group stronger and more bonded.

Token economy. A system of tokens (stars, checkmarks, chips, etc.) or points that students can exchange for tangible rewards and/or privileges. It may be classroomwide or set up for an individual student through a behavioral contract.

Trapping. Systematic, careful design of instruction to promote success. As a result, the student finds acceptance and motivation. Trapping also promotes teacher/student relationships.

Verbal de-escalation. Talking to students to help calm them down, regain control, and resume the activity or lesson. Crisis situations have several phases, and verbal interventions may vary depending on the phase. See the table on page 129.

Vignette. A short scenario that can be used as the basis for discussion of a particular behavior, social skill, difficult situation, etc. The vignette can be created by a teacher or student or be an excerpt from a book, short story, video clip, and so on.

Verbal Interventions

Phase	Student behavior	Teacher response
Anxiety	Student shows increasing anxiety; increasing motor or verbal behavior or unusually quiet and withdrawn behavior; mild disruption	Be supportive; don't use ultimatums; give hurdle help; help the student see the problem as solvable.
Questioning, ignoring	Student questions the teacher; student may ignore teacher direction.	Remain calm and businesslike; communicate clear expectations and stress the consequences of the desired behavior.
Refusal	Student overtly resists or defies the teacher.	Remain calm and avoid a power struggle; offer realistic choices; provide the student with an option that protects the student's dignity and allows face saving.
Emotional release	Student loses control; has little ability to listen or to reason at this point.	Provide support and safety. If the student is crying, provide support and empathy; if the student is verbally aggressive, minimize the damage to others (move them away) and talk soothingly to the student; if the student is physically aggressive, get assistance.
Tension reduction	The student generally withdraws; still needs time to regain self-control; may need to prepare self for consequences of the crisis situation.	Provide acceptance and support; assist the student to return to classroom activities when appropriate.

Source: Van Acker, Rick. *Verbal interventions with aggressive children and youth.* Retrieved September 19, 2003, from www.wm.edu/TTA/articles/challenging/verbal.html

References

Boeckmann, D., Cardelli, G., & Jacobs, J. (1989). *Alternatives for persons who are behaviorally challenged.* Crystal, MN: Hennepin Technical College, District #287.

Bullis, M., Walker, H. M., & Sprague, J. R. (2001). A promise unfulfilled: Social skills training with at-risk and antisocial children and youth. *Exceptionality, 9,* 67–90.

Chansky, T. E. (2000). *Freeing your child from obsessive-compulsive disorder.* New York: Three Rivers Press.

Cleveland Clinic Department of Psychiatry and Psychology. (2005). *Mental health: Causes of mental illness.* Retrieved October 31, 2006, from http://webmd.com/content/article/60/67140.htm

Connecticut State Department of Education. (1997). *Guidelines for identifying students with a serious emotional disturbance.* Hartford: Author. Available from www.sde.ct.gov/sde/lib/sde/PDF/DEPS/Special/SEDguide.pdf

Curtis, D. (2003). *Ten tips for creating a caring school: Raise your students' emotional intelligence quotient.* Retrieved December 28, 2007, from www.edutopia.org/10-tips-creating-caring-school

Gargiulo, R. M. (2004). *Special education in contemporary society: An introduction to exceptionality.* Belmont, CA: Thompson-Wadsworth.

Gresham, F. M., Sugai, G., & Horner, R. H. (2001). Interpreting outcomes of social skills training for students with high-incidence disabilities. *Exceptional Children, 67*(3), 331–344.

Hair, E. C., Jager, J., & Garrett, S. B. (2002, July). *Helping teens develop healthy social skills and relationships: What research shows about navigating adolescence.* Washington, DC: Child Trends. Retrieved September 20, 2004, from www.childtrends.org/Files/K3Brief.pdf

Hallahan, D. P., & Kauffman, J. M. (2006). *Exceptional learners: An introduction to special education* (10th ed.). Boston: Allyn and Bacon.

Hansen, D. J., Nangle, D. W., & Meyer, K. A. (1998). Enhancing the effectiveness of social skills interventions with adolescents. *Education and Treatment of Children, 21*(4), 489–513.

Hardman, M. L., Drew, C. J., & Egan, M. W. (2005). *Human exceptionality: School, community, and family* (8th ed.). Boston: Allyn and Bacon.

Harper, J. (2003). *Depression facts: What depression is not, what depression really is.* Retrieved May 4, 2005, from www.freedomhealthrecovery.com/depression.html

Heward, W. L. (2006). *Exceptional children: An introduction to special education* (8th ed.). Upper Saddle River, NJ: Merrill/Prentice Hall.

Hunt, N., & Marshall, K. (2005). *Exceptional children and youth* (5th ed.). Boston: Houghton Mifflin Company.

Individuals with Disabilities Education Act (IDEA), 34 C.F.R. § 300.8(c) (4) (2004).

Ishii-Jordan, S., & Peterson, R. L. (1994). Behavioral disorders in the context of Asian cultures. In R. L. Peterson & S. Ishii-Jordan (Eds.), *Multicultural issues in the education of students with behavioral disorders* (pp. 105–114). Cambridge, MA: Brookline Books.

Jensen, M. (2005). *Introduction to emotional and behavioral disorders: Recognizing and managing problems in the classroom.* Upper Saddle River, NJ: Merrill/Prentice Hall.

Kallam, M., Hoernicke, P. A., & Coser, P. G. (1994). Native Americans and behavioral disorders. In R. L. Peterson & S. Ishii-Jordan (Eds.), *Multicultural issues in the education of students with behavioral disorders* (pp. 126–137). Cambridge, MA: Brookline Books.

Kauffman, J. M. (2005). *Characteristics of emotional and behavioral disorders of children and youth* (8th ed.). Upper Saddle River, NJ: Pearson.

Kerr, M. M., & Nelson, C. M. (2002). *Strategies for addressing behavior problems in the classroom* (4th ed.). Upper Saddle River, NJ: Merrill Prentice Hall.

Kirk, S. A., Gallagher, J. J., & Anastasiow, N. J. (2003). *Educating exceptional children* (10th ed.). Boston: Houghton Mifflin.

Kochhar, C. A., West, L. L., & Taymans, J. M. (2000). *Successful inclusion: Practical strategies for a shared responsibility.* Upper Saddle River, NJ: Prentice Hall.

National Dissemination Center for Children with Disabilities (NICHCY). (2004). *Emotional disturbance: Fact sheet # 5.* Retrieved May 20, 2005, from www.nichcy.org/pubs/factshe/fs5txt.htm

National Institute of Mental Health (NIMH). (2001). *The invisible disease: Depression.* Retrieved May 5, 2005, from www.mental-health-matters.com/articles/article.php?artID=218

Office of Special Education Programs (OSEP). (2001). *The twenty-third annual report to Congress on the implementation of IDEA.* Washington, DC: U.S. Department of Education.

Peterson, R. L., & Ishii-Jordan, S. (1994). Multicultural education and the education of students with behavioral disorders. In R. L. Peterson & S. Ishii-Jordan (Eds.), *Multicultural issues in the education of students with behavioral disorders* (pp. 3–13). Cambridge, MA: Brookline Books.

Pierangelo, R. (2004). *The special educator's survival guide* (2nd ed.). San Francisco: Jossey-Bass.

Pierangelo, R., & Giuliani, G. (2006). *Assessment in special education: A practical approach* (2nd ed.). Boston: Allyn and Bacon.

Rosenberg, S. D., Mueser, K. T., Jankowski, M. K., Salyers, M. P., & Acker, K. (2004, May/August). Cognitive-behavioral treatment of PTSD in severe mental illness: Results of a pilot study. *American Journal of Psychiatric Rehabilitation, 7,* 171–186.

Salend, S. (2001). *Creating inclusive classrooms: Effective and reflective practices* (4th ed.). Upper Saddled River, NJ: Merrill Prentice Hall.

Shinn, M. R., Walker, H. M., & Stoner, G. (Eds.). (2002). *Interventions for academic and behavior problems II: Preventive and remedial approaches.* Bethesda, MD: National Association of School Psychologists.

Topper, K., Williams, W., Leo, K., Hamilton, R., & Fox, T. (1994, January). *A positive approach to understanding and addressing challenging behaviors: Supporting educators and families to include students with emotional and behavioral difficulties in regular education.* Burlington: University of Vermont, Center on Disability and Community Inclusion.

Turnbull, R., Turnbull, A., Shank, M., & Smith, S. J. (2004). *Exceptional lives: Special education in today's schools* (4th ed.). Saddle River, NJ: Prentice Hall.

U.S. Department of Education. (2001). *The twenty-third annual report to Congress on the implementation of IDEA.* Washington, DC: Author.

U.S. Department of Education. (2004). *The twenty-sixth annual report to Congress on the implementation of IDEA.* Washington, DC: Author.

World Health Organization (WHO). (2007). *International Statistical Classification of Diseases and Related Health Problems* (10th rev.). Geneva, Switzerland: Author. Retrieved December 30, 2007, from www.who.int/classifications/icd/en/

Wright, D. B., Gurman, H. B., & the California Association of School Psychologists/Diagnostic Center, Southern California Positive Intervention Task Force. (1994). *Positive intervention for serious behavior problems: Best practices in implementing the Hughes Bill (A. B. 2586) and the positive behavioral intervention regulations.* Sacramento, CA: Resources in Special Education.

Zins, J. E., Elias, M. J., Weissberg, R. P., Greenberg, M. T., Haynes, N. M., Frey, K. S., et al. (1998). Enhancing learning through social and emotional education. *Think: The Journal of Creative and Critical Thinking, 9,* 18–20. Available from www.casel.org/downloads/enhancinglearning.pdf

Index

CORWIN PRESS

Made in the USA
Lexington, KY
23 March 2014